FERMENTATION
& Home Brewing

FERMENTATION

&

Home Brewing

JESSICA CHILDS   &   ERIC CHILDS

STERLING EPICURE
New York

An Imprint of Sterling Publishing
1166 Avenue of the Americas
New York, NY 10036

ISBN 978-1-4549-1774-8

Distributed in Canada by Sterling Publishing
c/o Canadian Manda Group, 664 Annette Street
Toronto, Ontario, Canada M6S 2C8
Distributed in the United Kingdom by GMC Distribution Services
Castle Place, 166 High Street, Lewes, East Sussex, England BN7 1XU
Distributed in Australia by Capricorn Link (Australia) Pty. Ltd.
P.O. Box 704, Windsor, NSW 2756, Australia

For information about custom editions, special sales, and premium and corporate purchases, please
contact Sterling Special Sales at 800-805-5489 or specialsales@sterlingpublishing.com.

Illustrations by Alexis Seabrook
Photography by Bill Milne Photography, except p.117 by Eric Childs and p.144
Design by Lorie Pagnozzi

Manufactured in the United States of America

2 4 6 8 10 9 7 5 3 1

www.sterlingpublishing.com

THIS BOOK IS DEDICATED TO OUR TWO LITTLE
BOYS, RIDER AND PAXIS. OUR BLISS IS IN
EMBRACING THE TINIEST OF THINGS IN THE
PRESENT.

WHAT IF FERMENTATION IS AN ACT OF LOVE?
WHAT IF OUR TINY MICROBIAL PARTNERS
ARE WHISPERING FROM THE CROCK, "WE'RE
IN THIS TOGETHER. WE'VE GOT YOU."

CONTENTS

PART ONE ✱ FERMENTATION FUNDAMENTALS 11

PART TWO ✳ EAT 57

PART THREE ✳ DRINK 117

⤳ INTRODUCTION ⤵

The kitchen is a magical place. In our home, we spend most of our time in the kitchen. Well after the meal has settled and the dishes are done, family and friends like to linger—talking, laughing, and tinkering around. We are drawn to the kitchen, lured there to be close to what nourishes, uplifts, and keeps us healthy. We want to be where the energy is, where creativity is sparked, and where our minds can wander. Inhabited by the foods that support life (and foods that are *alive*!), the kitchen is the kinetic center of our home. And the engine—the heartbeat of our kitchen—is fermentation.

Our kitchen is in perpetual motion. Food and drinks bubble in jars and sigh in bottles as the evolutionary magic of fermentation prepares—and transforms—them. We celebrate our place within the ecosystem by bringing fermenting microbes into our home and allowing them to create the health-supportive and delicious foods that humans have evolved alongside and enjoyed throughout history.

Fermenting microbes are an extraordinary class of creature. A tiny army of bustling microscopic sous chefs, they have evolved culinary skills that humans could never even dream of mastering, skills that impart distinctive flavors, textures, and nutritive characteristics to simple, raw ingredients. These minuscule gourmands and the products of their efforts also valiantly protect our foodstuffs from spoilage more completely than any other preservation system we know.

You may recognize their names: mold, yeast, and bacterium.

If you have chopped a cabbage and squeezed it through your fingers, wringing out the moisture to provide the liquid for sauerkraut, or have thrown a SCOBY (Symbiotic Culture Of Bacteria and Yeast) into leftover wine to make vinegar, you know that microbes are tools, partners, and friends in the quest for creating robust and alluring live foods. Get comfortable using fermenting microbes and harnessing their potential for culinary greatness, and your kitchen will become a palette of colors, flavors, and ideas. You, the master artist, will be capable of turning just about anything that's fresh and within reach into unique ferments.

We have been fermenting things both at home and professionally for over two decades. In that time we have tried all sorts of things—putting fish in our sauerkraut, throwing a kombucha SCOBY into grape juice, making tempeh from soba noodles . . . Our list of experiments is endless. Along the way, the great lesson we have learned is: amazing things happen with food when you are armed with fermentation knowledge.

This book is the road map you need to confidently ferment to your heart's desire. With tried-and-true traditional recipes as a starting point, we will visit the staple ferments we like to make in our home kitchen.

Along the way, we'll take you down some side roads we discovered while tweaking our own unique ferments, like using yogurt to make cheese or tossing cashews into our kimchi to round out the flavor. You'll also find road signs in the form of sidebars. Keep these helpful guidelines and interesting points in mind while you embark on your own fermentation journey. Once you get the hang of it, you'll be mixing mashed potatoes into your pickles for a creamy, exotic condiment and dehydrating your yogurt for a popcorn topping. With the power of microbes on your side, the world of health and wonder is yours to explore.

THE WORLD IS YOUR CROCK

Our fermenting kitchen is not unique. People all over the world are looking to dig a little deeper into a rich (and delicious) treasure-trove of fermentation knowledge that has all but vanished in modernized societies in the wake of the industrial food revolution. Some of us are looking for ways to improve our health; some of us want to preserve the bounty of summer (and escape expiration dates) and perpetuate the techniques of our ancestors. Still others search for the flavors, textures, and nutrients that only fermentation can impart. Whatever draws you to fermentation, prepare to be changed by what you discover here.

Fermentation is a hub with spokes that intersect nearly every culture throughout history. The shared, evolving history of microbial and human partnerships is at the center of this common ground in all times and places. Fermentation is where past meets present, where we come together, where food becomes greater than the sum of its ingredients, and where man meets microbe.

THE ORIGINS OF FERMENTATION

Humans have enjoyed fermentation and put it to good use since ancient times. The impact of fermentation is just as momentous as other enormous eureka moments and inventions that have shaped civilization and mankind, such as fire, farming, and the wheel. However, the who, what, when, where, and why of its maiden voyage cannot be precisely pinned down. In fact, fermented foods were likely not "discovered" but were deeply intertwined with us all throughout human history. As you will discover later in the Introduction, man and microbe are not as separate as they may first appear.

As the history of fermentation is open to speculation, we are free to envision all sorts of possible ways in which some ancient, adventurous gastronome discovered a powerful ferment: A hungry honey harvester climbed a tree to shake a hive to the ground. Poor planning landed him in a pickle, so he had to promptly descend and run to save his hide from a thorough stinging. Upon his abrupt departure, he jostled the hive, which fell right into a puddle of fresh rainwater. A few days later, a thirsty traveler stumbled upon this puddle, now bubbly and sweet-smelling. She said to herself, "Boy, does that look refreshing," and thus enjoyed the first deep chug of the world's first mead. Imagine the feeling: the silky, floral flavor of wildflower honey mead followed by a warm, heady sensation traveling toward the fingers and toes as the low-level alcohol hit the bloodstream. Bliss.

Or envision this scenario:

A wild gatherer, returning to her shelter on a moonless evening after a day of harvesting wild greens, followed a path that meandered through a brackish wetland. She stumbled in her new leather shoes and dropped her tightly woven basket full of greens. She quickly bent down and retrieved her basket, but didn't notice that the basket had taken on brackish water. When she reached her homestead, she placed her basket in the larder, a cool earthen hole in the ground. A few days later, when she revisited the larder to have her first snack from the spoils of that day, she discovered the wonderful world of brine and lacto-fermented vegetables.

Regardless of the origins of fermentation, this technology is wildly significant in the history of mankind. The process of fermentation breaks down hard-to-digest foods and frees up the valuable food energy locked within. Fermentation protects wild-gathered, hunted, and harvested foods from spoilage and rot, and it creates key nutrients that keep human bodies robust and help fight infections. Alcohol, a by-product of many ferments, unleashes pleasurable sensations in the body and lubricates social life. It is no wonder that we see fermentation in almost every culture throughout history.

From ambrosial to microbial

Over the millennia, local fermented foods were carried far and wide from their native lands and shared from community to community and around the globe. The exotic new flavors spooned from earthenware crocks carried by wandering tradespeople were mesmerizing. People swooned at the heady sensations from grain beers that came from afar. And they struggled to understand just what magic was happening in their own fermentation pits.

Fermentation played a huge part in shaping human psychology, spirituality, and civilization, and a parade of gods was created under the influence of these perplexing and, at times, mood-altering foods. In fact, many scholars believe that fermentation was the catalyst for the formation of the first human settlements. As University of Pennsylvania archeochemist Dr. Patrick McGovern observed in his article published in the *Independent* on January 15, 2010, titled *Did a Thirst for Beer Spark Civilization?*: "A main motivation for settling down and domesticating crops was probably to make an alcoholic beverage of some kind . . . People wanted to be closer to their plants so this leads to settlement."

The Sumerians were among the earliest humans to develop a writing system, around 1800 BCE, during the Middle Bronze Age. An important cuneiform text from their literary canon, which still exists, is known as "A Hymn to Ninkasi." In this poem a female deity known as Ninkasi builds an entire town from scratch and then immediately sets about the essential task of fermenting the bread and beer, illustrating the relationship between civilization, spirituality, and fermentation.

*Ninkasi, having founded your town
upon wax, she completed its great
walls for you . . . Ninkasi, it
is you who handle the . . . dough
with a big shovel, mixing, in a
pit, the beerbread with sweet
aromatics . . . Ninkasi, it is you
who water the earth-covered malt;
the noble dogs guard it even from
the potentates . . . Ninkasi, it is
you who soak the malt in a jar; the
waves rise, the waves fall. Ninkasi,
it is you who hold with both hands
the great sweetwort, brewing it
with honey and wine...*

THE ELECTRONIC TEXT CORPUS OF SUMERIAN
LITERATURE (UNIVERSITY OF OXFORD)

Fast-forward a few thousand years to the nineteenth century, and Louis Pasteur—with the help of Antonie van Leeuwenhoek's compound microscope and Robert Hooke's *Micrographia*—ushered fermentation into a new time, where microbes were revealed to be both friends and foes. Pasteur was the first to discover the role that microbes play in fermentation as well as disease—a role that has confused mankind ever since, as we have oscillated between loving and hating our industrious microbial frenemies.

MAN MEETS MICROBE

During the twentieth century, the battle to come to terms with microscopic life drove the Western world into an era of germ-free living (or the illusion of it). Once consumers realized that some microbes were capable of causing disease, we became fearful of the entire population—whether there was probable cause or not. The subsequent development and marketing of processed, packaged foods and antibacterial soap created a false sense of security.

Armed with a rudimentary understanding of the role microbes play in our own health and that of our environment, we shed much of the knowledge that humans had gathered from millennia of living in partnership with microbes. Far too many fermentation recipes were lost as the industrial food revolution swept the globe.

Today, we are on the road to man-microbe reconciliation. A new vision of microbes is emerging, and it highlights partnership and interconnection. As this new understanding takes hold, it is becoming apparent that there is no separating man from microbe, nor should there be.

The number of microbes that exist on planet Earth is staggering—currently estimated at between 9.2×10^{29} and 31.7×10^{29}. There are about 10 million trillion microbes for every single human being on the planet. Like most biological entities, microbes are fierce niche-holders, steadfast in establishing territory for themselves and their kind to proliferate. As such, they have evolved some remarkable skills. From petroleum to rocks to caffeine to nuclear waste, they "eat" *everything*; from oxygen to nitrate to iron, they "breathe" *everything*; and from 252°F thermal heat vents on the ocean floor to 5°F permafrost in the high Arctic, they are thriving *everywhere*.

Microbes occupy a combined total of approximately 960 square feet of surface area on and in your body, and your microbiota (microscopic living organisms that inhabit you) can be found on every single inch of that area. The surface of your skin, only approximately 18 square feet of that total, is home to over a thousand kinds of microbes, including bacteria, fungi, and viruses.

The rest of your surface area—the vast majority of it, in fact—is inside your body: the sensitive epithelial tissues of the lungs, gastrointestinal (GI) tract, and vagina. As we repeat the simple acts of taking in oxygen from the atmosphere and expelling carbon dioxide, and consuming the nutrients that will become our body's building blocks and fuel, we interface with the environment and ecosystem more than we do when we roll around in grass or swim in a river. In short, our insides are swarming with microbes.

In fact, these hitchhikers outnumber human cells in our bodies by at least one order of magnitude, and the vast majority of them are nestled deep inside us. What are they doing in there? Just being themselves: multiplying, eating, getting rid of waste, partnering with some species, merging or fighting with others, and occasionally fighting with us.

Where does the environment end and the self begin?

As you consider what we know about our microbiota, you might start to wonder where the microbes end and you begin. An easy distinction to make between you and your microbial inhabitants might be that any cell that does not share your unique genome is not you. Dig a little bit deeper and you'll see this easy definition doesn't quite fit. Did you know that you actually carry two distinct genomes? There is the genome that we all know and speak of, that of the chromosomal DNA that you inherited from both of your parents. But in addition, we all have another separate genome that is less widely regarded: mitochondrial DNA. Mitochondria, as you may remember from high school biology, are tiny organelles that are in most of your body's cells. They have their own independent genome and their own methods of reproduction within your body's cells. In some form or another, mitochondria are absolutely essential to every life form . . . except bacteria, which do not have them.

So the lack of mitochondria distinguishes bacteria from all other life forms? What are mitochondria, exactly? That's the funny thing: they are ancient ancestors of ancient "bacteria," before bacteria had a name and the sea was awash with the first life forms: single-celled organisms. One of these single-celled organisms climbed inside another one, and they both made out like bandits in their symbiosis. From here, complex life as we know it was just a stone's throw away. So what are we? A highly sophisticated colony that resulted from a bacterial merger? Perhaps!

Let's look at the question of where microbes end and your body begins another way, from the perspective of autonomy and the higher functions, such as decision-making. It is now clear that our microbial hitchhikers influence our behavior by altering brain chemistry, development, and cognition. Scientists in labs worldwide are seeking to discover how your microbiota relates to your psychological health in conditions ranging from stress-related disorders such as depression, anxiety, and irritable bowel syndrome

to neurological disorders such as autism and Alzheimer's. Fascinating research strongly suggests that our on-board microbial population has more say in what we eat, how we eat, and when we eat than the entire mass of gray matter between our ears. Athena Aktipis, of the Arizona State University Department of Psychology, said in an August 15, 2014, article written for the UCSF News Center titled *Do Gut Bacteria Rule Our Minds*: "Microbes have the capacity to manipulate behavior and mood through altering the neural signals in the vagus nerve, changing taste receptors, producing toxins to make us feel bad, and releasing chemical rewards to make us feel good."

The implications of these findings are widespread and will definitely cause a few existential crises. Every day, our understanding of our own microbiota evolves, but one thing is clear, as science writer Carl Zimmer put it so eloquently in his article published in the *New York Times* on August 14, 2014, titled "Our Microbiome May Be Looking Out For Itself": "It's a lovely, invisible garden we should be tending for our own well-being."

With bodies whose vitality is largely dependent on their microbiota—and with microbes setting up shop en masse inside our gut—we are not only what we eat, but also *who* we eat, in a manner of speaking.

MAN'S NEW BEST FRIEND: THE HEALTH BENEFITS OF FERMENTATION

Just as complex life is the result of coevolution between archaic single-celled organisms, our very high-tech human body has evolved into our modern state alongside those same single-celled organisms. After all these years of living together, we have developed codependent relationships with our bacterial relatives. We are completely dependent on an appropriate balance and abundance of microbes in our gut for good overall health and for digestive efficiency.

In the quest to dominate their environment (or at least protect their turf), microbes participate in the normal activities one would expect. They eat stuff for energy and growth. They expel what they don't need. They procreate. They clean and maintain their homes. They respond to threats by deploying appropriate defenses. They socialize.

Our gut microbiota carries out these activities inside our bodies. It's been this way for millennia. As a result, our bodies have evolved to push certain tasks onto microbes, utilizing them for their special abilities. By harnessing their natural functions, our bodies use our microbiota to:

Increase our gut's absorption of water.

Break down energy sources our bodies would not otherwise be able to digest, like certain fibers, starches, and complex sugars.

Help our bodies absorb essential dietary minerals, like calcium, magnesium, and iron.

Do funny things that we don't yet understand, like altering the surface of individual cells along our gastrointestinal tract.

Enhance the integrity of the intestinal walls.

Produce a number of vitamins, like vitamins B and K.

Reduce, and in some cases, eliminate damaging bacteria that might otherwise

set up shop in our bodies, resulting in inflammation and infection.

Control and stimulate the replenishment of fresh GI tract cells.

Possibly interrupt cancer genesis and cancer growth.

Maintaining a specific balance of species in our microbiota is essential to good health. If our microbial community is disturbed, the results can be catastrophic. "Dysbiosis" is the term used to describe a disrupted and imbalanced internal microbial community. The result of dysbiosis is an increased susceptibility to all sorts of diseases that can affect the entire body. Intestinal disorders such as celiac disease, irritable bowel syndrome, and inflammatory bowel disease, and extraintestinal disorders such as cardiovascular disease, diabetes, asthma, and obesity are all linked to a poorly maintained microbiota. Dysbiosis also weakens the overall immune system, resulting in more respiratory and skin infections with more intense, longer-lasting symptoms. Inappropriate immunoreactions such as eczema and allergies also become amplified through dysbiosis. And, not surprisingly, dysbiosis is associated with higher rates of multiple types of cancer.

Repeated studies and analyses over many decades have shown that, although the precise mechanism is unknown, eating probiotic-rich foods has a significant normalizing effect on microbiota. Dysbiosis can be both prevented and reversed in many individuals by consuming fermented foods on a regular basis.

* * * * * * * * * * * * * * *

Some scientists have shown that very few live microbes, if any, actually make it past the stomach's highly acidic environment, which hovers around a pH of 2. But somehow the act of consuming live microbes remains the most effective tool we have to maintain a proper microbial gut population. It is thought that the microbes we eat send chemical signals down the digestive tract that inform and fundamentally change the population that has already taken up residence. Perhaps with all the gene-swapping that goes on in the microbial world, the genetic material (also an acid, DNA can withstand a relatively low pH) of live microbes makes it through the stomach and arrives in the gut to be incorporated. Whatever the mechanism, the beneficial results of eating probiotic-rich foods have been shown time and time again through numerous studies.

* * * * * * * * * * * * * * *

part one

FERMENTATION FUNDAMENTALS

chapter 1

∽ FERMENTATION 101 ∿

O n our planet, nothing is wasted. Microbes are the ultimate recycling crew, constantly sorting, deconstructing, and remaking the world anew. At the molecular level, nutrients are circulated around and around through plants, animals, slimes, molds, bacteria, fungi, and every other life form. When a leaf falls to the ground, it contains species-specific molecules that are then broken down and rearranged by microbial species into simpler, more universal compounds. Those nutrients can then be absorbed by another plant and used to build another leaf, one that an animal may come along and eat to build or fuel its body. Either way, matter is neither created nor destroyed, and microbes are incessant workers in planet Earth's organic-matter recycling strategy.

When it comes to fermenting, we harness this microbial breakdown process to create foods that have desirable flavors, textures, and aromas and tap into our heritage of coevolution with these species. We are drawn to the unique characteristics of fermented foods because we know intuitively that they offer enhanced nourishment and health-sustaining properties, and also help our bodies stay in balance.

Not all microbial processes result in a fermented food, however. You shouldn't reach into your compost and grab a rotten pear for a snack. Foods ferment under specific conditions, but most of these conditions are exceptionally easy to create, as you are essentially re-creating the environment in which these ferments would spontaneously occur in nature. By paying mind to six key environmental conditions—substrate, water, oxygen, temperature, pH, and microbial inhibitors (page 19)—you can cultivate specific microbes in your home fermenting kitchen to produce a wide array of delicious, colorful, and healthful fermented foods.

While a fermentation process unfolds, the conditions within the ferment shift. If more than one species is involved in a specific ferment, these shifts encourage different species to grow and proliferate at different times. For example, *Leuconostoc mesenteroides* is first on the scene in sauerkraut and pickle fermentations. It can initiate fermentation across a wide range of temperatures and salt/sugar concentrations, rapidly dropping the pH and increasing the CO_2 concentration to create the ideal anaerobic and acidic environment for the subsequent growth of the *Lactobacillus* species that finish the job. These changes not only promote the growth of desirable bacteria, they also inhibit the growth of unwanted spoilage and pathogenic microbial species.

WHO'S WHO IN THE WORLD OF FERMENTATION

With multitudinous recipes available for fermenting yummy foods, it might seem like there must be an equal number of food-fermenting microbes. In actuality, only a select few microorganisms ferment foods, and they all come from one of three categories: bacteria, yeast, and mold. Lucky for us, the desirable species are either abundant in our own natural environment or quite easy to obtain from reputable sources. Some of these cultures can be used over and over again, so once you obtain one, you will be able to make endless iterations of the same ferment. Once you know which microbes you are culturing, and what their preferred environments are, they are quite easy to cultivate, and the possibilities are endless.

Bacteria

Bacteria—amazing and complex single-celled organisms—have gotten a bad reputation since the invention of the microscope. Pasteur's discovery that the world was inundated with tiny life forms—bacteria responsible for a host of human, plant, and animal deaths and disease—was the beginning of a wave of fear and misinformation that reverberated around the world. And rightfully so. But as microbiology has advanced, we have learned that the vast majority of bacteria are not harmful and, in fact, are quite helpful and even necessary for a robust and healthy body. Humans and bacteria cannot be separated; we are inextricably bound together, and our mutual relationship is essential to our survival. Fermenting food with bacteria is a reconciliation of our partnership.

Because bacteria were the first life form on Earth (along with their microbial cousins, archaea), they have had plenty of time to evolve impressive abilities. Bacteria eat pretty much anything. From sugar to sunlight, from iron to oil spills, if there is a way to utilize it, bacteria probably do. The bacteria that we use in fermentation consume protein, fats, and carbohydrates and are categorized by the major outputs of this consumption—lactic acid and acetic acid.

LACTIC ACID-FORMING BACTERIA are the most widely used microbial type in food fermentation. They are involved in the fermentation of sourdough, beer, milks, cassava, and most vegetable ferments. Bacteria from the genera *Lactobacillus, Leuconostoc, Pediococcus*, and *Streptococcus* are the main species involved in lacto-fermentation, although several others have been identified as playing smaller roles.

The name "lactic acid–forming bacteria" can be deceiving. Although these bacteria are known for their ability to convert carbohydrates into lactic acid, it is by no means all that they do. As a group, these bacteria make a wide variety of compounds, from other organic acids to functional enzymes to small

amounts of alcohol. And like other fermenting microbes, they take the vitamins and other nutrients that are locked up in complex molecular "cages" within the substrate (the foodstuff or drink that will be fermented), and free them up, making them more readily available for digestion when consumed.

These lacto-fermenting bacteria occupy a wide range of niches in our natural environment, thus they can be used in a wide array of fermentation conditions. Thermophilic (heat-loving) species like *Lactobacillus delbrueckii* subsp. *bulgaricus* and *Streptococcus salivarius* subsp. *thermophilus* are most productive in the hot environments used in yogurt-making (see chapter 4). Mesophilic (room temperature–loving) species like *Leuconostoc mesenteroides* and *Lactobacillus plantarum* are perfectly suited to ferment at ambient temperatures and are key players in vegetable ferments such as pickles and kimchi.

Instead of using oxygen from the air for metabolism, lacto-fermenting bacteria use oxygen that is bound up in more complex molecules within the substrate. Although they can survive in the open air, in a field of cabbage for example, lacto-fermenting bacteria prefer low oxygen environments like those found in undisturbed liquids. When you make pickles, kimchi, or sauerkraut, you submerge your vegetable substrate below the surface of a liquid to create the environment that lacto-fermenting bacteria thrive in.

If you have a bounty of fresh vegetables that you need to store for longer periods of time than your refrigerator can keep them fresh, lacto-fermentation is the ideal method of preservation, as it keeps them safe, vital, and crispy and even increases their healthfulness.

ACETIC ACID-FORMING BACTERIA are the second group of bacteria important to home fermenters. As their name suggests, strains from the *Acetobacter* genus produce mainly acetic acid, which is the acrid, strong, and yet delicious flavor that is characteristic of vinegars. Although *Acetobacter* strains are not prominent members of the human microbiota, the molecules they form are a central metabolic component of the human gut. *Acetobacter* cells are ubiquitous in nature, especially in or near places where alcohol is produced: for example, the nectar of flowers, damaged fruit, and wineries, of course.

Vinegar fermentations, which usually begin with a fruit juice but sometimes grains or vegetables, are actually a two-step process. The first step involves yeast and the production of alcohol. The *Acetobacter* then feeds on the alcohol to make acetic acid. Both steps can happen in what seems like one step if you use a SCOBY, because the SCOBY introduces both the yeast and the *Acetobacter* to the substrate, and as soon as alcohol is made, it is immediately converted to acetic acid. This happens when you make kombucha or apple cider vinegar. Or the process can happen in two distinct steps; for example, when you make red wine vinegar, where first the wine is made with yeast, and then *Acetobacter* is added to consume the alcohol, lowering the pH. Once the pH has significantly dropped due to the increase in acetic acid, the yeast activity is killed and the ferment kicks into high gear, creating an abundance of acetic acid. Both alcohol and acid inhibit the growth of food-spoiling and pathogenic microbial species, so at both steps in the process the substrate is protected from spoilage.

Yeasts

Tiny single-celled fungi, yeasts are responsible for the fermentation of two of the world's favorite things: bread and alcohol. Food-fermenting yeasts, like certain species of *Saccharomyces* and *Candida,* feed primarily on glucose, but some feed on other plant-based carbohydrates like maltose, sucrose, and raffinose. They are prolific in the natural environment and are found in high concentration around their favorite foods: in orchards, vineyards, and fields of grain. They are also residents of the digestive tracts of many animals, where they have a constant, steady supply of these foods. Some fermented products are made using only yeast: beer, wine, grain alcohol, and some breads (in which yeast leavens). Other yeast-fermented products are actually a collaborative effort between yeast and bacteria: sourdough bread, kombucha, kefir, and vinegars.

Yeasts are easy to grow, as they are active in a broad range of temperatures and can tolerate some acidity. Most require at least a moderate amount of oxygen, which is why they are largely excluded in lacto-fermentations, where oxygen levels are low, and in aceto-fermentations, such as the second step of vinegar production, once the *Acetobacter* start using up all the oxygen and the level becomes exceptionally low.

Yeasts can utilize the sugars in fruits straight off the tree or vine, but they cannot break down the sugars in cereal grains, as they do not produce the necessary starch-breaking enzyme. Therefore, yeast can ferment wine directly from grapes, but to make beer, the starches must first be broken down in a preliminary step, such as malting (germinating by soaking the grain in water).

* * * * * * * *

Occasionally, yeast can become pathogenic to humans. The pathway to diseases such as thrush, athlete's foot, vaginal yeast infections, or various yeast-driven skin disorders is not well understood, but it is generally agreed that these diseases occur in patients with compromised immune systems or a distinct hormonal profile, such as occurs during pregnancy. In general, yeasts are a very obedient part of the human microbiome. But in instances where yeast proliferates uncontrollably in the body, health practitioners urge patients to stay away from yeast-fermented products. Bacteria-based ferments can help to re-establish a proper balance of microbes in the microbiome, but you should consult your health-care provider, because the underlying cause will need to be established.

* * * * * * * *

Molds

Mold fermentation is not as common in the West as bacteria and yeast fermentation, but mold ferments are nutritionally and gastronomically exquisite and worthy of a place in the home fermenter's kitchen. Some of our favorite ferments utilize the special skills that mold has perfected and that transform substrates into easily digestible, earthy-flavored, and soft-textured delicacies. Familiar foods like miso, blue cheese, sake, and tempeh are all based on mold fermentation, or have a mold fermentation component. In Asian societies, mold has been widely used for centuries to make a largely grain-based diet easier to digest. Molds produce the greatest array of enzymes of all the fermenting agents, making them ideal for breaking down hard-to-digest grains and legumes. The same powerful mold enzymes are used in ways as various as food and biofuel production, cleaning up oil spills, and other highly specialized biotech applications.

Like bacteria and yeasts, mold spores are ubiquitous in nature and in the home environment. Molds are tolerant of a wide range of conditions and therefore play a large role in food spoilage. If you leave a raw cabbage out on your countertop, undesirable mold will eventually reduce it to a crumbling pile of mush. However, the heartiness of mold works to the home fermenter's advantage, as desirable strains are surprisingly easy and safe to cultivate.

In our home fermenting kitchen, we use *Aspergillus oryzae* and *Rhizopus oligosporus* mold strains to break down grains and legumes. If you want to make mold-ripened cheese, *Penicillium candidum, Penicillium roqueforti,* and a host of other cheese-ripening strains can be used. All these molds require a good amount of oxygen to proliferate. This distinguishes mold ferments from all other ferments; molds simply cannot survive in low-oxygen settings the way fermenting yeast and bacteria do (there is some amount of oxygen dissolved in most liquids). Some people think the term *fermentation* should not be used to describe an oxygen-rich mold transformation in food, citing that, scientifically, the term refers to anaerobic respiration. But in the context of home fermenting, the term is widely used to describe any microbial transformation of foodstuffs.

Mold ferments are most often part of a more complex fermentation process. In miso, sake, and cheese, for example, mold fermentation is a preliminary step that is then followed by a secondary bacterial or yeast fermentation. Most cultures you will find for making viili, a Scandinavian dairy ferment, have a mold component that proliferates on the oxygen-rich surface of the milk while the lactic acid–forming bacteria and yeast do the lion's share of the work under the surface in the mostly anaerobic liquid environment. The result is a velvety smooth top layer above the viscous and acidic viili.

Tempeh, however, is purely fermented with mold. Softened, dehulled beans and/or grains are inoculated with a mold strain, often *Rhizopus oligosporus*, and incubated, resulting in a brick of thick mold bound tightly around and throughout the beans. Not only is the tempeh brick a true culinary gem in shape, texture, and flavor, but mold enzymes have destroyed certain indigestible compounds—and compounds thought to have deleterious health effects.

CURATING THE ENVIRONMENT

Let's say it again: Microbes are everywhere. Mold spores that will utterly destroy a great summer cucumber sit side-by-side on a cucumber's skin with beneficial, lactic acid–forming bacteria. So what is the difference between a moldy cucumber and a delicious, crispy pickle? The environment! If you leave a cucumber uncovered on a warm countertop, you've given undesirable mold spores a one-way ticket to the front of the line for their next meal. Mold loves lots of oxygen and warm temperatures, so a warm kitchen counter is a wonderful place for mold to rot food. But if you take that same cucumber and cut off its air supply, the mold will just sit there idly while its microbial neighbors—the beneficial bacteria—have

their heyday of food, festivity, and lacto-fermentation. One of the simplest ways to cut off air supply and curate the environment for lacto-fermentation is to simply submerge the cucumber under liquid. This restricts the air supply that mold needs to grow and creates an anaerobic environment that lacto-fermenting bacteria thrive in.

Furthermore, you can fine-tune your ferment by adjusting the conditions in other ways. For instance, if you take your submerged cucumber down to your cool-temperature root cellar, certain lacto-fermenting bacteria will be dominant for a longer time, the fermentation will happen more slowly, and the result will be a crisper pickle than if you had left it on your warm kitchen counter.

The home fermenter tinkers with six conditions when creating microbial magic:

substrate

water

oxygen

temperature

pH

microbial inhibitors

Each fermentation type will thrive within a certain range of each of these conditions. If you take a particular fermentation type out of its comfort zone, other microbes will take the opportunity to claim territory, and you may wind up with undesirable results. But if you stick within the correct range, your desired microbes will reward you.

Armed with the answers to the fundamental questions underlying fermentation, you will understand the inner workings of traditional recipes and be able to use their concepts freely to develop fresh takes of your own. The recipes in this book are designed to get you started with the different types of home fermentation, and each one has directions to help you provide the optimal conditions for success.

SUBSTRATE

A substrate is the foodstuff or beverage that will be fermented. We haven't come across anything natural that you can eat that you can't ferment. In fact, there are some foods that are healthful only after they have been fermented. Worldwide staple foods like cassava and soybeans fall into this category. Vegetables, fruits, grains, seeds, nuts, beans, milk, eggs, fish, meat, and every other foodstuff you can think of can be fermented, as long as it doesn't have fermentation inhibitors (discussed below).

* * * * * * * *

Cassava, a starchy tuber, is native to South America, but its territory has grown to include Africa and Asia with the help of human industry. Some varieties of cassava have copious amounts of cyanogenetic glucosides, which convert to cyanide when you chew them. These toxic varieties have been cultivated for consumption for over ten thousand years and are consumed only after a fermentation process renders them innocuous.

* * * * * * * *

Fermenting microbes differ in their nutritional requirements and their preference for different substrates. Nutrient requirements for the various fermenting agents vary from simple sugars to more complex carbohydrates, and some even prefer proteins. Since these microorganisms require very high quantities of certain nutrients, they tend to colonize substrates with a high degree of specificity. For a lacto-ferment, that may be milk or vegetables. For the mold ferment tempeh, the substrate will be beans, grains, or seeds. For wine, a yeast ferment, the substrate is fruit juice or honey.

What happens when the substrate isn't ideal for a particular microbial species? The microbial community that ferments kombucha, for instance, thrives off the nutrients in the tea and sugar solution that has become the standard recipe used by most kombucha makers. With a little tinkering, we discovered that you can inoculate all sorts of things with a kombucha culture, with varying results. If you inoculate a crock of grape juice with a kombucha culture, for instance, it will make a tasty jug of bubbly fermented grape-juice "soda" that kids love to drink on a sunny afternoon. But that kombucha culture will not propagate in grape juice for more than one or two rounds of fermentation, because grape juice has some, but not all, of the nutrients kombucha needs. It may also contain other compounds that kombucha microbes aren't as comfortable in. Kombucha will never be a robust grape juice fermenter, but it is fun to do as a side project every once in a while with a spare SCOBY. If you put a SCOBY into unsweetened tea, there may be enough residual sugar in the SCOBY for it to feed off for a few hours, but eventually this essential ingredient will run out, and you will be left with a flat ferment.

Water

Water is the potion of life—all life. It is essential to every cell on the planet, no matter where it is, plant or animal, single-celled or multicellular, floating in the air or submerged deep in the ocean. When fermenting something, you manipulate the moisture content of the substrate to discourage unwanted microbial growth and encourage the right organisms to proliferate. When you lacto-ferment vegetables, you submerge them in water or some other water-based liquid. But if you want to curate the right environment for *Rhizopus oligosporus* to ferment beans into tempeh, you'll want to dry all but a small amount of the water off the beans, as the mold needs only a small amount of moisture to thrive, and will drown if there is too much. If the conditions are not sufficiently dry, the mold spores will stand by idly while some other, unwanted microbe devours the substrate. In our experience, this particular mistake results in crumbly tempeh that stinks of ammonia.

In addition to pouring or straining off water, there is another, subtler way to manipulate the amount of water available for microorganisms. The addition of sugar or salt binds up some of the water molecules and makes them unavailable to microbes. We do this when we submerge our summer cucumbers, using a brine—or mixture of salt and water—instead of pure water. The addition of salt binds up some of the water, inhibiting undesirable microbes while still keeping the available water within a range that *Lactobacillus* (the main lacto-fermenting microbe) can thrive in.

WATER ACTIVITY AND MICROBIAL GROWTH

Water Activity (a measure of the water available for microbes)	Species Affected	Examples
1.00		Distilled water
0.99		Fresh meat and fish Highly perishable foods
0.95	Some yeasts and some pathogenic bacteria inhibited	Fresh bread Foods with 40% sucrose or 7% salt
0.90	Salmonella, Vibrio parahaemolyticus, Clostridium botulinum, Lactobacillus, and some yeasts and fungi inhibited	Lower limit of lacto-fermentation Foods with 55% sucrose or 12% salt
0.85	Many yeasts inhibited	Aged Cheddar cheese Foods with 65% sucrose or 15% salt
0.80	Lower limit for most enzyme activity and growth of most fungi	Soy sauce Fruit syrups
0.75	Lower limit for halophilic (high salt concentration–tolerant) bacteria	Fruit jams
0.60	Lower limit for all osmophilic (high sugar concentration–tolerant) and xerophilic (low water activity–tolerant) yeasts and fungi	Dried fruits (15–20% water)
0.55	DNA molecules become disordered	Lower limit of water content for life to continue
0.50		Most dried and freeze-dried foods

Oxygen

All life forms utilize oxygen. But where they get that oxygen from differs. Humans and trees "breathe" free oxygen from air. Some microbes do something similar, taking their oxygen from the air around them too, but others utilize oxygen that is molecularly bound to other compounds like carbohydrates. Broadly, we can classify all our fermenting microbes as either aerobic or anaerobic. Aerobes grow well with access to oxygen. We are aerobes! So are fish, which remove free oxygen directly from water. In contrast, anaerobes thrive in the absence of free oxygen, utilizing the oxygen or other elements bound up in a substrate's molecules for their metabolic processes.

The majority of ferments that we home fermenters make utilize yeast and bacteria. This means that under most circumstances, mold growth will be contamination. But rest assured, if you have an anaerobic environment—either by liquid submersion, air lock, or seal—mold cannot grow. And when your conditions aren't perfect and some mold growth does occur, it will be only on the surface of your ferment in contact with air. Mold will never grow underneath the surface of a liquid.

Perhaps the most profound lesson on the oxygen requirements of microbes is this: mold cannot grow in the absence of oxygen. So if you see something funny floating inside, under the surface of your kombucha (or kefir, wine, etc.), it is yeast, not mold.

Temperature

All living cells and creatures are affected by temperature. Our DNA encodes proteins that are dependent on certain temperature ranges in order to function. If the temperature gets too warm for a particular organism's proteins, those proteins denature (or unwind) and the organism will die. If the temperature gets too low, the proteins' activity decreases or halts, and the organism either dies or goes dormant.

One of the factors that makes microbial species so successful, evolutionarily, is that they have been able to adapt to a wide range of temperatures. Thermophilic species, like *Streptococcus salivarius* subsp. *thermophilus,* used to ferment yogurt, like it hot. Psychrophiles can live in extreme cold, some even in frozen conditions like *Chryseobacterium greenlandensis,* which was found alive after 120,000 years buried in a glacier.

The largest group, the mesophiles, likes temperatures in the same range we do. The microbes that ferment our foods mostly reside in the mesophilic category, but some are thermophilic and require a little bit of effort to be kept thriving in the home kitchen.

As your fermenting practice progresses,

keep in mind that microbes behave in subtly different ways near the higher or lower extremes of their optimum temperature range. Toward the higher ends of a temperature range, the fermentation process tends to speed up, destroy more of the crispy structure of the substrate, and create stronger flavors: when kombucha ferments at a higher temperature, the acetic acid–forming bacteria are more active, resulting in a stronger vinegar flavor. This is ideal when you are going for the zing that makes condiments perfect by the teaspoon. Toward the lower temperature end, the fermentation happens more slowly and the final ferment winds up with a smoother flavor, where subtler characteristics can shine through. For example, traditional kimchi is fermented mostly at the very low end of the mesophilic range, often in root cellars, in refrigeration, or even buried in the cool earth. This allows the crispness of the vegetables and the delicate flavor combinations to come forward. Another example of this temperature difference is in lager beers, where fermentation is carried out at lower temperatures than most other beer types, resulting in a smooth, crisp finish.

Room temperature is an expression used to describe the range of temperatures that are considered preferable indoors. If you are comfortable in either a long sleeve or short sleeve cotton shirt, you are mostly likely within that range. On a thermometer, room temperature is loosely between 68°F and 75°F.

pH

Put simply, pH is a measure of how many hydrogen atoms are floating freely in a solution. Unbound hydrogen atoms are highly reactive, and all things, living things included, have ranges of tolerance for them. In fermentation, this is a great tool, as we can manipulate the pH of our substrate to encourage the ferment that we want to take place.

The optimum pH for the majority of microorganisms is around 7 (neutral), the pH of pure water at room temperature. A small amount of acidification will take the water out of the comfort zone of most microorganisms. But not the comfort zones of the beneficial acetic acid–forming and lactic acid–forming ones we use for food fermentation! Acidification of water is yet another way to ward off the growth of unwanted species and tilt the scale in the direction we want it to go: toward beneficial fermentation. Some ferments, such as kombucha, benefit from the added protection of acidification of the substrate right from the start. That's why the kombucha recipe calls for adding some already fermented kombucha at the start, along with the SCOBY.

Other ferments, like lacto-fermented raw veggies, generally don't need this help as the pH rapidly drops a few hours after the fermentation process has begun. One very beneficial effect that pH has on a lacto-ferment is that, as the fermentation progresses, the pH continues to drop, becoming more and more acidic. In the beginning of the fermentation process, when the substrate has only just begun to acidify, certain bacterial strains get busy creating more acid, thus lowering the pH. As the pH drops, it exceeds the tolerance range of those initially active species, and they subside, allowing more acid-tolerant species of bacteria to proliferate. The result is an ever-changing microbial landscape throughout the life of your ferment. Eating your veggie lacto-ferment in the beginning of its fermentation cycle, for example, will introduce a different probiotic population to your body than if you ate that same ferment on day three. Day three will be still different from day five, and so on.

MICROBIAL INHIBITORS

There are two kinds of microbial inhibitors of note in home fermenting. First are the inhibitors that might be added to the ferment as an ingredient. Ginger, thyme, cinnamon, and honey have their own antimicrobial properties that can attenuate or even stop some types of fermentation from taking place. Even salt and sugar can become microbial inhibitors when used in high concentration, as discussed above in the section on water. Once you are comfortable with what a specific ferment looks like, acts like, and smells like when it is progressing smoothly, you can experiment with ingredients that may inhibit growth. You'll know pretty quickly if your ferment is not doing so hot, and if you've used a microbial inhibitor as an ingredient, you'll know why. Once we tried to ferment ginger-spiced noodles with *Rhizopus oligosporus* for a nice tempeh. It didn't work. Only a few sparse mold filaments grew, and we wound up with an undesirable, off-smelling pile of gingery noodle mush. The ginger actually inhibited the *Rhizopus* mold from growing. Another example is our experimentation with chai tea kombucha. Some chai mixtures ferment into delectable, healthful kombucha. Other mixes result in a liquid with an unpleasant odor and weak SCOBY growth. We speculate that some blends are heavier on the cinnamon, a known microbial inhibitor, than others. In our experimentation, we have seen that there is usually a threshold for the amount of an inhibitor that can be added before it starts to affect the ferment. This threshold is different for different inhibitors and for the various microbial species. For example, if you mix a good amount of ginger with sugar and water, it lacto-ferments into what is called a ginger bug, which can be used to make all sorts of fermented sodas. But that same ginger, used in a much smaller proportion, is what killed our tempeh in the example above.

The second kind of microbial inhibitors are created by the fermenting agents themselves. In the microbial world's constant state of war, beneficial microbes use them as an arsenal of tools to ward off the growth of other, perhaps undesirable, species. These microbial inhibitors are also part of what makes eating fermented foods so healthful. They do the same job in your body that they do in your ferment: ward off unwanted microbial growth, protecting you from infection and microbial disease.

chapter 2

✷ THE FERMENTER'S PANTRY ✷

To make an omelet you have to crack an egg. You also need a certain set of specialized tools: a hot skillet, a spatula, a rich fat to cook with, and your chosen ingredients. When you have everything you need, the perfect omelet is possible. As you set out into the world of fermentation, the right ingredients and tools are essential for creating fermentation masterpieces, and may be the difference between culinary genius and culinary disaster. Don't worry, though; it's likely that many of the tools you need are already in your kitchen. If not, most can be found at your local grocery or hardware store. A select few are available only in specialty fermentation supply stores or online. In general, many of your favorite ferments can be made with everyday culinary tools.

INGREDIENTS

Fermentation enhances the nutritive qualities of food, unlocking some nutrients, creating others, breaking down difficult-to-digest compounds, and adding the unanalyzable essence of live food that only microbes can contribute. The most nutritive, robust, and delicious ferments begin with the most nutritive, robust, and delicious ingredients.

Choose organic foods when you can. Organically grown foods are produced by farmers and processed by organizations that have shown that they do not use bioengineering, ionizing radiation, or most conventional fertilizers, antibiotics, growth hormones, and pesticides. Free of chemical residues, and expressing time-tested genomes that have not been tampered with, organic foods have been shown to be safer and healthier for you, your family, your community, and your environment. Not to mention, they are far more delicious!

Choose local when you can. The nutrients in all foods begin to degrade the moment they are picked from the vine. Just after harvesting, fresh fruits and vegetables begin producing enzymes that degrade their color, flavor, and nutritive qualities. Processing, packaging, shipping, customs, and handling all take up valuable, nutrient-depleting time. If you can, find a local farmer or Community Supported Agriculture (CSA) program that can provide you with fresh meat and very recently harvested produce.

If you can access only conventionally grown, nonlocal, or canned ingredients, fermentation will certainly enhance their nutritive qualities. So ferment away! But keep in mind that their native microbial population may not be as robust. In canned foods, all the microbes will have been annihilated in the canning process, so such food should only be incorporated into ferments with other non-canned foods or heavily inoculated with an established culture.

* * * * * * * *

Don't knock frozen foods! If local produce isn't available to you, consider the benefits of buying some frozen organic produce. Flash-frozen hours after picking, frozen fruits and vegetables are often more nutrient-dense than their fresh counterparts on store shelves. Freezing preserves many of the vitamins that rapidly degrade, while deactivating many of the enzymes responsible for their destruction. However, freezing will also deplete the native microbial population of your raw produce, so you will have to take that into consideration when setting up your ferment by either mixing them with raw live microbe-containing ingredients or an already established culture.

* * * * * * * *

FERMENTATION VESSELS

Many types of vessels for fermenting food are available. Some are designed to facilitate a specific type of ferment. Others may be useful for a range of fermentation applications. You can also make a number of aesthetic choices along the way.

When searching your cupboard or your favorite local shop for a fermentation vessel, consider the following questions.

What am I going to ferment?

You will need to know this before heading out on your gathering expedition. What you choose to ferment will greatly inform your answers to the next questions and the type of vessel you will choose.

What shape should I use?

When it comes to vessel shapes, there are many to choose from. If you will be tightly packing shredded veggies for a lacto-ferment or slinging balls of inoculated beans to make a fine and mellow miso, choose a vessel with an opening that is at least as large as your fist. If you will be sealing off a liquid with an air lock, you will need a shape that accommodates your equipment, like a jug-shaped carboy sealed with a rubber stopper called a bung.

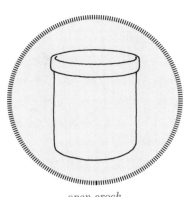

open crock

carboy

What are its oxygen requirements?

Consider how you will curate the environment to contain oxygen (aerobic) or allow the oxygen to be displaced (anaerobic).

Oxygen-rich ferments are not difficult to set up, as the open air is the preferred environment for the fermenting agent. Simply covering your kombucha or kefir crock with a tightly woven cloth will keep out most of the pests that you will encounter, such as fruit flies or excessive mold spores.

On the other hand, anaerobic ferments are happiest in environments that have no oxygen, so these need a little bit more preparation. The oxygen that contacts the surface can cause trouble in the form of mold or yeast growth on the surface. Again, unwanted mold or yeast will grow only on the surface where the oxygen is, although molds can shoot usually innocuous filaments down under the surface of the liquid as they scavenge for nutrients. Many home fermenters are not concerned with these unwanted fungi growths on their ferments and will just scrape off the top layer and discard it before jarring up and devouring the contents below. In our home, we try to minimize this growth. For one, if you have fungus sensitivity, the filament growth down into the solution may affect you. Even if you scrape off the top layer, some of those fungi will be swept under and into the ferment. For the most part, these fungi are not harmful. But the main reason we strongly avoid this practice is because the surface growth imparts an off-flavor to the ferment that our highly tuned, fermented food–loving palates pick up on instantly.

swing-top jar with
rubber gasket

How, then, can you limit this unwanted surface growth and set up a proper anaerobic environment? During the fermentation process, lots of new gases will be formed, bubble up through the surface of the liquid, and need to escape. If the vessel allows these gases to escape but does not allow outside air to get back inside (conditions you can create with an air lock), carbon dioxide will quickly displace the oxygen in the airspace above the substrate in the vessel. Oxygen levels under the surface of the ferment are not a factor when setting up lacto-ferments as they are already quite low from the start, and the small amount of dissolved oxygen is rapidly displaced with CO_2.

If you are making an anaerobic ferment like sauerkraut, it is easiest to use vessels like Fido jars, which have a rubber gasket and swing-top lid. Another option is to use a jar with a tight-sealing lid, like a mason or Ball jar, outfitted with a rubber gasket and air lock.

There are also a variety of specialized options for anaerobic food fermentation, such as the Harsch crock, which has a lid that forms a seal when filled with water. These crocks have been wonderful for us when setting up long-term anaerobic ferments, such as hatcho miso, which has a two-year fermentation time. The only hitch is that you have to check the crock regularly to ensure the water does not evaporate beyond the critical level and break the seal you are relying on. For shorter ferments like shiromiso, we have found the water seal to be too messy, and other vessels do the same job without the mess.

water-filled bag
used as weight

Still another option for anaerobic fermentation is a regular jar with a regular lid. Let the lid sit on the jar loosely during fermentation to allow gases to escape. Some people advocate using a thin film of oil on the surface of the ferment to "seal" the environment from oxygen. We aren't comfortable recommending this process due to the possibility of botulism hiding within the oil layer. We have found no definitive information that offers a conclusion one way or the other. We do like, however, to put a clean glass or ceramic fermentation weight, a sealable plastic bag full of water, or even a clean boiled rock on top of the substrate. This puts pressure on the substrate, holding it under the surface of the liquid, if submerged in liquid as in brined vegetables, and helping to expel any air pockets below the surface. It also keeps surface area and air movement above the ferment minimal. For misos, and other thick ferments such as condiments, a thick layer of salt on the surface will keep unwanted aerobes from setting up shop. If you can remember to do it, instead of out-fitting your veggie lacto-ferment, such as pickles or kraut, with a weight, you could just remove the lid and disturb the surface every day to keep any fungi spores that have landed there from growing. To do this, lightly splash a clean fork all around the surface daily, stirring the liquid on top and applying gentle pressure to release any built-up gas bubbles in the substrate. That should do the trick. Make sure to replace the lid.

How large a batch do I want to make and how much space do I have for this project?

Before you go out and buy the biggest crock you can find, make sure your family and roommates are willing to accommodate this new adventure. We have heard of many domestic disputes arising from a home fermenter's growing passion. And remember, if you make a whole bunch of fermented stuff, then you must store it. Is there room in your fridge for five gallons of sauerkraut?

How much money do I want to spend?

You don't have to spend a dime on a vessel to get started with your first fermentation. Regular jars such as mayonnaise, salsa, or pickle jars will do the trick, and if you don't buy any of those items, head to the local deli, which will certainly have used pickle jars to recycle for your purposes. Also check out local thrift shops, where vessels gather for repurposing. Just make sure that your vessel is made to hold food. Some materials can leach harmful chemicals into food, so if it is not clearly marked as a food vessel, either call the manufacturer or pass on it.

What aesthetic, if any, am I going for?

Whether it's beautiful blue swing-top bottles, post-steampunk stainless steel, or earth mother ceramics, go for the material that makes you feel good! There are few things that are sweeter in life than arriving at a potluck with the best-looking dish for the table.

No matter what vessel type you choose, be sure to clean it thoroughly before filling it. A good scrub in a hot soap bath with a sponge or bottle brush will be sufficient for many ferments. Some of the more delicate ferments, like single-strain yeast beers and wines, may require that the bottles be sterilized before filling. Refer to specific recipes for more information on this.

Glass

Glass fermentation vessels are a beautiful and safe choice that not only provide the perfect container for your ferment, but also offer a window into the magic. Glass is the material we use most. Once you are familiar with the ferments you love making, you can tell just by looking at them how far along they are. When choosing a glass jar, consider the process of setting up your ferment. If you will be working with a hot liquid, like the brewed tea substrate of kombucha, make sure to use only jars that are suitable for canning. If the ferment will likely build up pressure, consider that as well. Ball, mason, and Fido jars all go through an annealing process that makes them able to withstand heat and pressure better than untreated jars. But even annealed jars can succumb to heat and/or pressure after multiple uses, so we always run jars under hot water for about thirty seconds to warm them up before filling them with boiling liquid. This seems to help. If you are working with hot materials but do not have a properly annealed jar, do the hot work in a pot or other stainless steel vessel and transfer it to the glass only once the liquid is properly cooled.

If you are using a glass vessel without a pressure-relieving system, like an air lock or a rubber gasket with swing-top lid, be sure to monitor the fermentation and relieve the pressure regularly. Otherwise you may end up with a mess on your countertop and a ferment contaminated with glass. In fact, I have heard reports of violent explosions occurring with glass shards scattered several feet around the room. This would be highly unlikely with a lacto-fermentation, but if you are bottle-conditioning a beverage in glass, we recommend doing so in a cardboard box or a cupboard where damages will be limited.

Glass Jars

There are quite a few options for glass fermentation jars. In fact, it's likely that you already own perfectly adequate fermentation jars if you regularly buy pickles, salsa, mayonnaise, or a variety of other foods from your local supermarket or other food stores. Ball jars, mason jars, or any glass vessels made for holding food can easily be repurposed as fermentation vessels. Also, with the rise of DIY fermentation, there are lots of options on the market that are perfect for home fermentation. Almost any glass vessel you desire can easily be found online, from half-gallon to three-gallon containers with various opening sizes, closures, and other design elements. Because glass is the most fragile material for fermentation vessels, keep in mind that the larger the vessel, the more fragile it will be, so use caution when cleaning and moving the vessel around. The largest glass jar we have ever seen in a store was a whopping five gallons. Refer to the above discussion in this section about oxygen requirements for more things to consider when selecting glass jars.

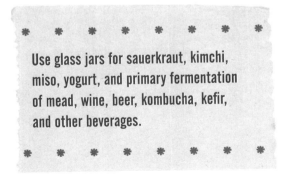

Use glass jars for sauerkraut, kimchi, miso, yogurt, and primary fermentation of mead, wine, beer, kombucha, kefir, and other beverages.

carboy with air lock

growler

Glass bottles

Bottles in the home fermenter's pantry are typically used for secondary fermentation and to store fermented beverages. They go by a variety of different names that loosely correlate to their size. Growlers are bottles in the half-gallon to one-gallon range. Carboys are larger bottles, usually in the five- or six-gallon range. Demijohns are the largest of the three vessels, usually holding around fifteen gallons. All these bottles have wide bases and trunks that taper sharply to a small neck and opening. They are designed with secondary fermentation in mind; their shape reduces overhead airspace, and the small opening is easy to plug. Smaller glass bottles are more affordable and are much easier to handle. Once you start getting into carboys or demijohns, a dedicated space is a must and your other equipment requirements, such as liquid transfer pumps, funnels, and more, will be greater as well. Not to mention the final yield will be enough for a pirate's wedding!

Once you make a vessel airtight by screwing on a lid or crown-capping a bottle, any fermentation that occurs within the vessel can become a ticking bomb as gas pressure builds. We use large plastic storage bins or even cardboard boxes to safely store our unpasteurized brews once they are sealed up in bottles or jars for bottle conditioning.

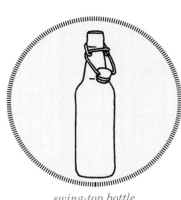

swing-top bottle

You can also reuse glass bottles that you've purchased. Used beer, soda, juice, wine, and tea bottles will help your budget and give you the satisfaction of knowing you are lowering the carbon footprint of the bottle.

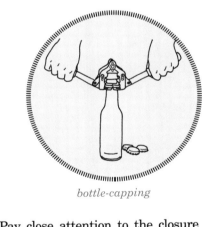

bottle-capping

Pay close attention to the closure on your bottle. If your ferment will be undergoing secondary fermentation to achieve carbonation, you will need to find a bottle with a cap that has a tight seal. Crown cappers and caps can be inexpensively purchased from any home brew shop for commonly used twelve-ounce beer or soda bottles, and they work well for secondary fermentation. Swing-top bottles are also good choices for secondary fermentation. Twist tops are hit-or-miss for ferments that build up carbonation. If you find a style with a good seal, use it! If you are just looking to store wine or a still beverage after fermentation, wine bottles with corks or regular mason-style jars are great.

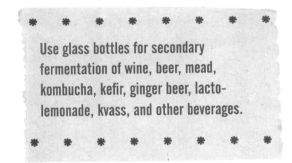

Use glass bottles for secondary fermentation of wine, beer, mead, kombucha, kefir, ginger beer, lacto-lemonade, kvass, and other beverages.

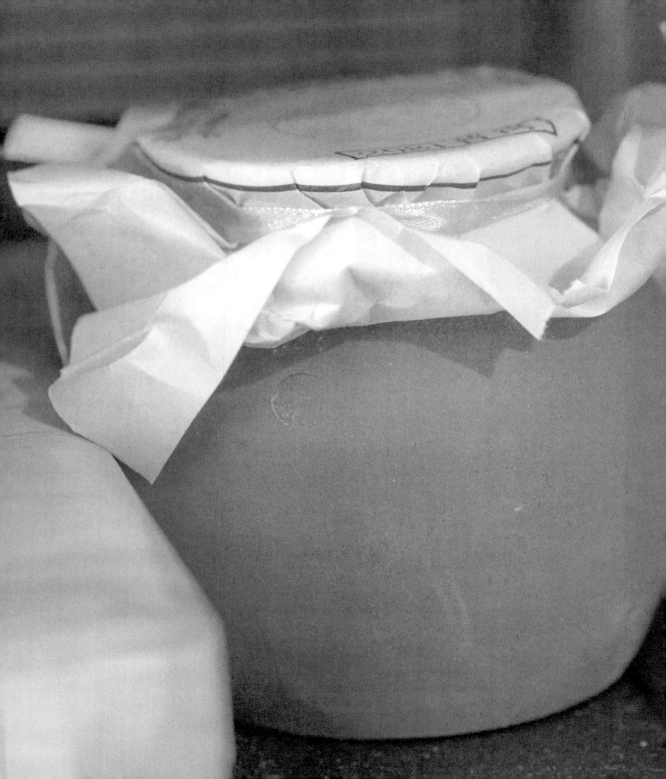

Ceramic vessels

Ceramic is the most widely used material throughout history for food and beverage vessels, including those used in fermentation. Nicely glazed ceramic remains one of the best choices for durability, safety, and aesthetics. Long ago, ceramic vessels were used for all forms of fermentation. While today, ceramic is used for food fermentation more than for beverage fermentation, it is still a great option for a lot of primary beverage ferments.

open-air crock

water-lock-style crock with weight

The most common shape of ceramic vessel that you are likely to run across is the crock. There are two main styles of crocks: the open-air crock and the closed-top water lock style, made popular by the German ceramic company Harsch. Each has advantages and disadvantages.

The open-air crock will need to be covered during fermentation with a tightly woven cloth, a plastic bag, a large plate, or something similar to keep out unwanted pests like fruit flies and excessive fungi spores. Open-air crocks have a nice wide mouth for easy packing, and they also make your ferment easy to check on throughout the process.

The closed-top water-lock crock has a channel that the lid rim sits in. The channel is then filled with water to create a seal that allows gases inside the crock to escape but prevents outside gases from entering. This arrangement is ideal for long-term ferments like cooler-temperature sauerkraut or hatcho miso, as long as you remember to check the water level periodically to ensure the seal is unbroken. This means no tasting throughout or peeking inside to monitor progress, as it is difficult to open the lid without dripping some of the stagnant, dusty water into the crock. When the time comes to open the crock, at the estimated end of the fermentation process, it is useful to siphon off the water or soak it up with a cloth first. For shorter ferments like room-temperature lacto-veggie ferments or shiro-miso, we find this style of crock with the water seal unnecessary and more mess than it is worth.

Both styles of ceramic crock are beautiful and safe to use, as long as the glaze is of recent food-grade quality. Some decorative-ceramic manufacturers use lead-based glazes, and some older food-grade ceramics were produced with lead. If your food-grade ceramic was made by a reputable stoneware company in the last twenty-five years, you should be good to go, but it never hurts to ask the manufacturer directly. Also, an easy-to-use lead test kit can be purchased from most hardware stores.

Ceramic is sturdy but can still be broken and is generally quite heavy. Vessels range in size from one gallon all the way up to twenty gallons. Prices vary, but new closed-top crocks are always more expensive than open-air ceramic vessels.

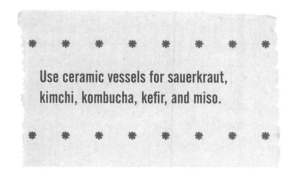

Use ceramic vessels for sauerkraut, kimchi, kombucha, kefir, and miso.

Plastic vessels

It is a common misconception that all plastics that are smooth and hard are food safe. But this is not so, and many people unknowingly misuse plastics perhaps to the detriment of their health. One big mistake people make is thinking any plastic marked with a recycling number is food grade. Not true! Another common belief is that all high-density polyethylene (HDPE) products are food grade. This is also false.

Although plastics do make for convenient and easy food containers, consider that the vast majority of plastics are not biodegradable. Or at least they won't completely degrade in any natural process that we know of. They may break down to very small particles, but then those tiny pieces enter the bodies of animals (humans included!) and wreak havoc on their endocrine systems. And then the plastics still don't degrade. If the animal is eaten by another animal (or slaughtered for human consumption), the toxic plastics move into the next body.

We strongly encourage you to avoid using plastic vessels for fermentation, if at all possible. We advise the use of plastics in a few of the beverage recipes, such as fermented sodas, the first few times you make them, so that you can measure the progress of the ferment and know when it is time to move the finished beverage to the fridge. Once you get the hang of a particular ferment with particular ingredients in your environment, you should be able to recreate it in glass and know when to move it to refrigeration, avoiding plastics altogether. If you do use plastic, use it sparingly and reuse containers as often as possible instead of purchasing new ones. For food and fermentation, use only plastics that are clearly labeled "food safe." If in doubt, ask the manufacturer.

Stainless steel vessels

Generally speaking, if you are looking at stainless steel, that probably means you are setting up a serious fermentation space. Stainless steel vessels are typically used for liquid ferments. More often than not, home fermenters turn to stainless steel only for advanced wine- or beer-making, but stainless steel is perfectly suitable for any number of ferments.

Fermentation-quality stainless steel vessels are made of pure, high-grade 304 stainless steel. Most kitchen cookware is made from a base of a lower-grade amalgam of metals and is only lined with 304 stainless steel. Such cookware is not well suited for fermentation because it scratches easily and therefore quickly corrodes in the acidic conditions that most ferments create.

Stainless steel vessels made specifically for fermentation are available in conical or cylindrical styles. Conical vessels are used by beer brewers and allow spent yeast cells to settle and pack tightly on the bottom as they fall out of fermentation, while providing the maximum surface area at the top for the oxygen that live yeast loves. They range in size from ten gallons to pretty much as big as you can imagine.

Cylindrical vessels are used more commonly for wine, kombucha, or other beverages, but some commercial operations specializing in other fermentation styles, such as lacto-fermented veggies, have found a good use for them too. Do your homework before you buy, and don't forget that used stainless steel is just as reliable as new but can be half the price!

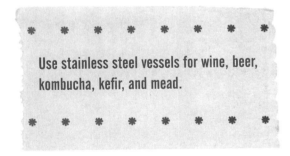

Use stainless steel vessels for wine, beer, kombucha, kefir, and mead.

Air locks

These helpful little devices are tightly wedged into the cap of a fermentation vessel and create near-perfect anaerobic conditions.

An air lock allows building CO_2 to escape, relieving pressure, while keeping the environment inside safe from outside air, which contains oxygen and potential contaminants. An air lock is essential for any sensitive ferment, like beer or wine, and can be used in a variety of other applications as well, such as lacto-fermented veggies. Air locks are usually wedged into the lid or opening of a vessel using a rubber gasket. Rubber gaskets and bungs can either be the size of the jar or bottle opening or can be wedged into an appropriate-size hole drilled in the lid of a wide-mouth jar. Air locks, rubber gaskets, drilled bungs, and even jar lids modified to accommodate air locks can be purchased at home brew shops and online.

TEMPERATURE CONTROL

Ferments are typically forgiving about temperature . . . within reason. When a ferment is allowed to unfold within its preferred temperature range, not only should you have no problems, but the ferment will be delicious. With just a little preparation, though, you can maintain consistency to a few degrees within that range and make truly exquisite ferments. Some people get scared away when considering how to maintain an environment's temperature. They haven't yet realized how easy it is. In most cases, no specialized equipment is required.

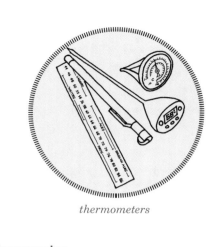

thermometers

Thermometer

Thermometers have two applications in fermentation. First, they are often used when you are heating and cooling a substrate prior to inoculating it, as is the case with miso—the soybeans are boiled, then cooled—or yogurt—the milk is heated to denature the proteins, then cooled before adding the culture. For this purpose, an instant-read thermometer that you can stick directly into the substrate comes in handy. There are sometimes ways around using an instant-read thermometer, though, and recipes in this book that have these types of heating and cooling steps will give alternate suggestions, when applicable.

The second use of thermometers in fermentation is to monitor the temperature of the substrate during fermentation. There are many ways to do this. Thermometers that stick to the side of the vessel are ideal. We use adhesive temperature strips frequently in our home for this purpose. Ambient thermometers also work well and can be placed right next to your fermenting vessel, giving you a close approximation of the internal temperature of most ferments. Digital ambient thermometers are available in hardware stores, easy to use, and quite affordable.

warming ferments

Towel or blanket

Maintaining a consistent temperature in an environment that fluctuates small amounts can be as simple as wrapping a towel or blanket around the fermentation vessel. It will act as a buffer, so when your warmly heated winter kitchen gets a little cooler at night, your ferment will maintain a steady temperature. Keep in mind that fermentation itself produces a small amount of heat, so wrapping your ferment in a thick covering in an already

warm room will further increase its internal temperature.

Lightbulb

Put your hand next to a light that has been on for a few minutes. Hot, right? Capture that heat and you have yourself an easy DIY temperature controller. All you need is a cardboard box, your ferment, a pendant light cord, and a lightbulb. When you put the lightbulb into the box, make sure it is at least five inches away from the fermentation vessel so it does not burn the contents and also five inches away from the cardboard; the box will need to be a good bit bigger than your vessel. For energy efficiency and/or cooler surrounding conditions, cover the box with a blanket or towel. Be sure to check the temperature of your fermentation chamber periodically to make sure you are in your ideal temperature range. Another modification on the lightbulb heating scheme is to include a thermostat (page 45).

QUICK TRICK: Your oven with the oven light turned on makes a great fermentation chamber. Just don't forget to put a sign on the front letting people know what you have going on inside. The last thing you want someone to do is to preheat your kombucha to 375°F!

heat mat and bottle

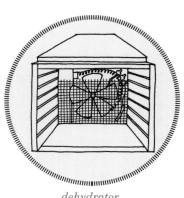

dehydrator

Heat mat

A cost-effective and easy solution for maintaining the proper temperature within your ferment is a simple heat mat purchased from a pet supply, gardening, or home brew shop. Heat mats are available in a variety of different sizes and wattages and can be placed directly under your fermentation vessel or inside a box or your oven, as described under "Lightbulb" (page 43), or you can simply wrap it around your jar or bottle. Whatever approach you take, keep an eye on the temperature for the first twenty-four hours to make sure it is within the range you are shooting for. Also consider adding a thermostat to this setup, described in more detail below (page 45).

Dehydrator

A dehydrator comes fully loaded with a heat source, a wind source for aerobic fermentations, and an internal thermostat. Most dehydrators have a limited temperature range just above the temperature in which mesophiles thrive. They work great for making thermophilic yogurts and *amazake*, but the internal thermostat cannot maintain lower temperature ferments such as tempeh. For lower-temperature ferments, we recommend bypassing the internal thermostat by plugging the dehydrator into an off-board thermostat, described below (page 45).

Central air control

If your house has central air control—the Rolls-Royce of temperature control in the mesophilic range—there's not much to do here but set your thermostat and walk away. You have a built-in temperature control. Even so, it might still be a challenge to convince your roommates or family that it's a good idea to keep the house at 88°F for the next day or so while you ferment the perfect batch of tempeh!

Thermostat

A thermostat paired with a heat source is not a bad thing to have on hand for all sorts of ferments, especially in the winter. Once you have a thermostat, you can plug it in to any number of heating elements, and the good news is it's not going to break your fermentation budget. Go to your local pet store and buy a twenty-dollar reptile thermostat. Some models have a dial setting with an unspecified range between high and low, and others are clearly marked with specific temperatures. With the former, you will need to monitor your setup with a separate thermometer until you to get to know where on the dial your ideal temperature is. When you find it, mark it with a permanent marker or a piece of colored tape.

If you have a dehydrator or yogurt maker, a thermostat with a limited range is likely built in. These work great for some ferments. But for others, the temperature range is too high. We use a dehydrator modified with a thermostat to maintain temperatures that are below the range of the dehydrator's internal thermostat. Of course, when you tamper with the way an electrical appliance is intended to work, you may be adding a level of risk—and most probably the action voids the manufacturer's warranty. If you are concerned, contact a licensed electrician.

FERMENTATION TASTING AND TESTING

This is an important section for the ambitious beverage fermenter. Most food ferments and beverage ferments are comparatively low-maintenance and don't require these sophisticated tools. But if you are inspired to make highly specific beers, wines, meads, and other beverages, it will require you to take samples along the way for specific things like acidity, specific gravity, or sugar content. As you become more comfortable with these ferments, the tools listed here will not be necessary each time, but they are invaluable for setting up standards and getting to know the fermentation process when you are beginning.

pH

The pH of your ferment will not only tell you how far along in the process your ferment is, but reassure you that your ferment is safe. The lower the pH of your ferment, the less likely unwanted growth will occur. This relationship is described in more detail in the pH section of Chapter 1: Fermentation 101. To determine the pH of your ferment, you will need either a digital pH meter or pH strips. Meters are a little pricey and need calibration now and then, but they will give you very accurate readings. While pH strips are a little less reliable, keep in mind that fermentation is generally safe as long as the environment is kitchen clean, so they are perfectly adequate for this job. The strips will turn a specific color corresponding to the pH range of your ferment. They are a budget-friendly and perfectly acceptable way to get to know the acidity of your ferment.

Brix refractometer

A refractometer reads the sugar content, or Brix, of a solution. Typically used in beverage ferments like kombucha, wine, and water kefir, a Brix refractometer won't set you back too much (about thirty dollars for a decent model) and will tell you exactly how much sugar, or sweetness, remains in your brew to help you decide when fermentation is complete or if you should let it go a few more days. If sugar content is something you need to monitor closely, as is the case for diabetics, people on the GAPS diet, or people who are especially sensitive to sugar, a refractometer will be a useful tool.

Hydrometer

If you are making alcohol, you will want a hydrometer to analyze your ferment's alcohol content. A hydrometer is used to test the specific gravity of a solution in comparison to that of water and comes with a handy chart to determine the alcohol content of your brew. Hydrometers are inexpensive (around ten dollars), found at any home brew store, and very accurate. Along with the hydrometer, you will need a cylindrical beaker to pour your sample into.

PREP TOOLS AND UTENSILS

Not to be overlooked when you are gathering your fermentation supplies, good prep tools will save you time and become essential in preparing your ferments just the way you like them. There is nothing worse than finding yourself in front of ten pounds of whole beans that need cracking with not a grain mill in sight.

Timer

Many ferments have steps that take a specific amount of time. Beer, wine, kombucha, and anything that involves steeping or mashing will need precise timing. A timer will help you get the job done. Most smartphones have timers built in, but we still like the kind

you wind up and leave on the counter—they reduce the risk of getting distracted by other bells and whistles along the way!

Knife

A knife is a chef's most important tool. Most kitchens already have one, but you'll want to consider having your knives sharpened to make crisp slices. We keep a honing steel on hand and run our knives across it every time we use them to keep the blades sharp.

Sharp knives are far safer than dull ones. With a dull knife, you need to apply a dangerous amount of pressure to do the same work a light touch with a sharp knife does. The amount of pressure it takes to get a dull knife through a cabbage makes slipping more likely, and that's when accidents happen. With a sharp knife, you are in control.

Grain mill

A grain mill is not a common kitchen item, but if you get into using whole grains and beans in your fermentation projects, this tool will become essential. For beer, you'll use a grain mill to crush the malted barley and expose the starch and enzymes that are within. For tempeh, you could use a grain mill on a very large setting to split the beans, and the hull will pop off in the process. Many home brew shops will have a mill available for you to use, but having one on hand means you can do this anytime, day or night, without having to wait in line.

Slicer

If you have ever tried to make a large batch of sauerkraut, then you will know why a slicer comes in handy (pun intended). Instead of cutting pounds and pounds of veggies by hand, grab a slicer—also called a mandoline—from a kitchen supply store. Use different attachments to dice, slice, or shred. A mandoline is a must for the avid veggie fermenter. And if you find yourself using the slicer often, invest in a chain-mail glove to protect the most important tool in the kitchen: your hands!

Strainers, colanders, and cheesecloth

Many ferments and related recipes require the removal of liquid somewhere in the process. A large mesh strainer or regular kitchen colander will work well in most cases. But when you want to strain the fine sediment from a ginger beer or kvass, or drain the whey from yogurt or viili to make a soft cheese, you'll want to line a colander with a few layers of cheesecloth for a finer sieve.

Spoon

How will all the ingredients for your ferment get mixed together? Your power combined with the power of a mixing spoon. Plastic, metal, and wood will all do the job, but due to the fragile nature of glass and ceramic fermentation vessels, we usually reach for wood.

Along with ceramic, wood has had a place in the home kitchen throughout history. If it is naturally treated and free of toxic chemicals, wood is a safe and lovely material to use in food preparation, but the constant demand for wood products has placed a huge burden on fragile ecosystems, and the dangers of deforestation cannot be overemphasized. When purchasing wood for your home, choose items that have been made using sustainable and green production practices. From cutting boards to coat racks, wonderful things are being done these days with intelligently forested bamboo. To protect our natural environment, avoid tropical hardwoods, such as mahogany and teak; avoid redwood, Douglas fir, and most western cedars as well.

Measuring devices

You will want to have a variety of measuring cups—dry and liquid—and measuring spoons on hand. These tools will be useful when you are following the recipes in this book for the first time and when you are measuring out ingredients that you can't measure by taste, like gochugaru (Korean hot chili flakes). Be sure to match the size of the measuring device to the batch size that you are working with. There is nothing more tedious than measuring a gallon of water with one-cup pours or more daunting than trying to estimate $\frac{1}{32}$ of a teaspoon.

Masking tape

One fermentation project is pretty easy to keep track of in your head, but keeping track of more than one gets a little iffy. A cabinet full of bubbling crocks and jars will start your head spinning. An easy workaround, if you don't have the mind of a World Memory champ, is simple masking tape. Use it to label each and every ferment you make with the start date, ingredients, temperature range, estimated completion date, or anything else you wish to track. Masking tape has saved us more times than we can count.

"Um, when did I start that again?"

"It was the day after your mother was here

and the day before I gave Rider that haircut that made him look like a punk rocker."

"Right . . . When was that?"

A typical label in our house looks like this:

CIDER	TYPE OF FERMENT
Gala/McIntosh	Ingredients of note
ECY/PE/N	English Cider Yeast/Pectic Enzyme/Nutrients
P 5/24/11	Primary fermentation start
S 5/27/11	Secondary fermentation start

Kitchen towel

A kitchen towel, or side towel, comes in handy not only to wipe up any spills on the counter or leaks down the sides of bottles, but to quickly clean your hands while processing veggies or measuring ingredients. Dedicated, hot water–cleaned towels are a must when you are working with ferments that require higher degrees of sterility, such as beer and wine. Clean, hot water–washed kitchen towels can also be used to dry the substrate in tempeh-making, and we also use them to wrap baguette dough while it is resting and rising.

Auto-siphons and racking canes

Transferring liquid from one vessel to another is one of the most difficult things you will do in beverage fermentation. When you are fermenting on a large scale (anything bigger than two gallons), pouring will not be an option. Trying to toss around a five-gallon crock full of kombucha is not only physically hard but dangerous—for the ferment and your back.

For transferring fermented liquids, an auto-siphon is the perfect tool. Both quick and easy to use, an auto-siphon is a tube construction that is pumped to create a siphon action. Auto-siphons often come built with

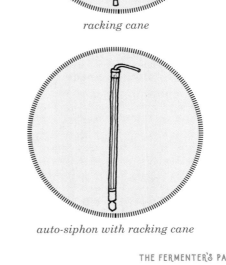

racking cane

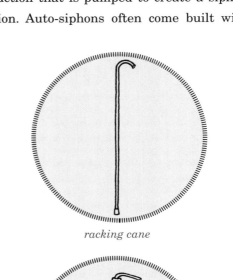

auto-siphon with racking cane

racking canes inside. Racking canes are long tubes, usually made from glass, with an opening ¼- inch above the sealed end. The racking cane transfers liquid while leaving behind any yeast or sediment—called *lees*—on the bottom. Some beverages, such as beer or wine, will require racking, so an auto-siphon with a built-in racking cane is a necessity in these instances.

A hose made from food-grade vinyl can become a simple siphon. Using the power of gravity, you can easily move liquid from one place to the next with this device. Just like in science class, you will put one end of the hose in the vessel you are transferring the liquid from. This vessel will be higher than the vessel you are transferring the liquid to. Once one end of the hose is situated in the first vessel, you can start a siphon by applying a gentle suction to the other end.

Sample thief

Samples of liquid ferments are often taken for tasting and testing during fermentation, to aid in determining doneness or when/if additions will be included along the way. A sample thief is a handy way to take samples of your liquid ferments while they are fermenting with little risk of contamination by unwanted microbes. Essentially, a sample thief is a long glass or plastic pipette with a tapered end that is dipped a few inches into the liquid. The other end is then closed using a finger, and the sample can then be removed. Sample thieves are stocked in brew shops and can also be found online. You will need a pipette cleaner or thin bottle brush to clean your sample thief. If you are working with sensitive ferments such as beer, you will need to clean the sample thief with sanitizer (as you would any other equipment used in the recipe) before use.

PEST CONTROL

Your friends and family are not the only ones who sniff around the kitchen in search of delicious food. Your ferments are prime targets for all sorts of unwanted species, from molds to black bears waking up from hibernation. Don't fret; with a few simple precautions, pests can be thwarted.

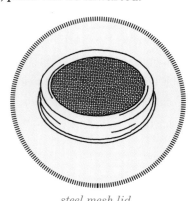

steel mesh lid

A friend of ours living in the woods in the Catskill Mountains once came home to find a black bear rummaging around in her kitchen! The bear was more startled than she was, and it ran off into the woods before eating all her kimchi. Consider the unique space you are working in, and protect your ferments appropriately. Field mice can chew right through cloth covers; a better approach in a country house might be a cloth covered with a steel-mesh lid (the kind used for growing sprouts).

cloth cover with rubber band

Cloth covers

In most fermenting kitchens, a ferment requiring oxygen (such as kombucha or kefir) will be well shielded against disaster by a fine-mesh cloth cover held secure with a large rubber band or ribbon. Any cloth that has a tightly woven mesh will do. Think about the size of the smallest insect that might wander into your kitchen, and make sure the weave is smaller. In a bind, even old T-shirts, side towels, or a paper towel can keep critters out while allowing oxygen to flow in. Cloths can be washed and reused until the weave has loosened. If you are using a paper towel, replace it if it gets wet. Regular cheesecloth does not work for this purpose, as the weave is too loose; even a fairly large fruit fly can navigate cheesecloth. However, butter muslin, a type of cheesecloth with a tight weave, does the trick.

In a pinch, cover your open-air ferment with a plastic bag tightly held to the sides by a rubber band. It won't be pretty, but it will get the job done!

Fruit fly traps

Fruit flies are the most common pest to infiltrate and destroy a fine ferment. An easy-to-construct fruit fly trap near your fermenting space will help protect your work from this very common annoyance. Take an empty bottle and add a few tablespoons of vinegar. Place the narrow end of a funnel or taped paper cone into the opening of the bottle and let it sit near your ferment. Flies will be attracted to the vinegar, enter the bottle, and get trapped in Davy Jones's locker at the bottom of the bottle. Only one of these DIY fruit fly traps will protect your entire fermentation chamber. Change the vinegar when there are several flies at the bottom or when the vinegar evaporates.

SANITIZATION

Most of the fermentation projects you will make in your home kitchen will require only a home-kitchen level of cleanliness. A gentle, nontoxic countertop spray cleanser will be perfectly acceptable for cleaning your countertops prior to setting up your yogurt, miso, tempeh, kefir, and kombucha ferments, for example. However, some ferments require a greater level of sanitization. Read the recipes in the book carefully for more information about the sanitization requirements of the fermentation you are starting. Single-species beverage ferments are not as resilient as those that utilize communities of microbes working in partnership, so ferments like beer and wine often require greater levels of cleanliness.

Cleanser

Cleansers are used to clean your surfaces, utensils, and vessels prior to setting up your fermentation project. In most cases, the sprays and soaps you already use in your home kitchen are enough to do the job. When a higher degree of sanitization is required, as in the case with most beer and wine recipes, you will use a cleanser before you use the sanitizers discussed below.

Sanitizer

A few styles of fermentation require a very high degree of sanitization in and around the fermentation space to protect a highly specialized microbial population from being overrun by ubiquitous environmental microbial species. For example, many beer and wine recipes have been developed to utilize single strains of yeast or a few specific strains of bacteria and yeast in combination to produce highly specific results. Contamination with the microbes naturally present on your kitchen counter might produce acidic beer or wine that tastes more like vinegar—in short, results that aren't quite what you were going for. For these more sensitive recipes, once your surfaces, tools, and fermentation vessels are thoroughly cleaned, they will need to be sanitized. Rinse and no-rinse sanitizers are available at all home brew shops. Powdered Brewery Wash (PBW) is the standard for cleanliness in the home brewer's prep space and can be bought at any home brew shop. Once the vessels are sanitized, keep them upside down on sanitized surfaces or racks to avoid airborne, microbe-containing dust particles from falling into them. Use gloves, wash your hands often, and take precautions to keep them sterile. The biggest overlooked source of contamination for the home brewer is your cell phone! Put your phone on airplane mode until you've arrived at your fermentation destination.

OTHER HELPFUL ADDITIONS IN BEVERAGE FERMENTATION

As we have gotten more and more sophisticated with our beverage fermentation technology, we have devised ways to hone the flavors and other characteristics of our brews while also optimizing our use of resources. By feeding the microbes optimum nutrition, helping them to break down tough-to-crack substrates, or just tossing in flavoring agents, brewmasters worldwide are able to create signature brews with subtle but distinctive qualities worthy of awards.

Nutrient boosters

The substrate of a beverage ferment is usually already packed full of nutrients, but some fermenting microbes may require an extra boost to carry them past the finish line to bring home an exquisite brew. In most cases, the use of nutrient boosters is optional, but some highly specialized and complex ferments require them to achieve optimum results. The most common boosters are yeast nutrients that are used in making beer, mead, and wine, and a few of our recipes in the Drink section make use of them. Inquire at your local home brew shop for more information on the many uses of nutrient boosters.

pH adjustors

Just as the name says, pH adjustors can impart an extra kick of acid or can bring back a ferment that is on the brink of undrinkability due to too much acid. Citric acid, tartaric acid, and acid blends can be used to increase the acidity of a yeast-dominant beverage. Potassium bicarbonate and calcium carbonate can be used to subdue an overly acidic finish. These can be purchased at your local home brew shop and include instructions for use. We rarely have had the need to use pH adjustors in our home fermenting kitchen. When a ferment turns out too acidic, we use it as a salad dressing or to deglaze pans, or we just drink it in small amounts mixed in with other things (think Arnold Palmer). The addition of acids may come in handy for perfecting the flavor profile of a wine, for example, in which the sugars, alcohol, and minerals can suppress the taste of acid on the palate.

Wine tannins

If you wind up with a dull, overly astringent, or undesirably bitter wine, tannins can balance and improve the flavor. Again, we don't use these in our home fermenting kitchen, because we can generally make use of bitter and astringent wines in cooking, or we just turn them into vinegar with the addition of some raw apple cider vinegar. But you can buy tannins at home brew shops and online if you were really counting on consuming your wine as wine.

Pectic enzyme

Used primarily in wine- and beer-making, pectic enzymes (or pectinase) break down the structural carbohydrate called pectin that is found in most fruit. Pectins are great in cooking, especially in jam- and jelly-making, for their tendency to form gels. However, this tendency can be detrimental in beer and wine, resulting in sludgy and cloudy ferments. Adding fruit to beer during fermentation can also result in clogged air locks. To prevent all these things, we often add pectic enzymes, available at home brew supply shops and online, which ameliorate the pectin problem and result in crystal-clear ferments.

part two

EAT

"AS ONE EATS KIMCHI, ONE EATS THE UNIVERSE AND,
IN SO DOING, BECOMES PART OF THE UNIVERSE, AND THE
UNIVERSE BECOMES A PART OF MAN."

—ANONYMOUS

chapter 3

∽ SAUERKRAUT, PICKLES, AND OTHER ∽ LACTO-FERMENTED VEGETABLES

Vegetable fermentation and preservation using lactic acid–forming bacteria is passed down in the recipe heritage of pretty much every society on the planet. Some well-known examples are German sauerkraut, which is actually an adaptation of an earlier Chinese ferment involving cabbage, and Korean kimchi, which was historically made with radishes and lacked the red pepper that was eventually introduced once Asian societies began trading with South American societies. It's a small world after all, brought even closer when looked at through the microbial lens. Read more about lactic acid–forming bacteria (lacto-fermentation) in Chapter 1: Fermentation 101.

What we love about lactic acid–forming vegetable ferments is directly related to what we love about the robustness of summer produce. Very few things are as pleasing as a walk through a garden in the height of summer. Lush leaves brush against bare legs. Sensual colors slow you down and make you look more closely. When you get up close to a perfectly ripened orb, plucking it from its stem is a small satisfaction bested by its lively symphony of taste and texture on the palate. We can bring this produce into the kitchen and, through lacto-fermentation, keep the vibrancy of a fresh living food well into the leaner months of fall and winter. A

crisp vegetable ferment set up during the fruitful months will bring back the pleasure and nutrients of summer throughout the colder months . . . with a tangy zip!

In an example of the synergies inherent in nature, vegetables come straight off the stalk lushly coated with the microbes that produce a fine lacto-ferment. As long as your raw vegetables aren't grown on Mars or in a completely sterile environment, they are already thoroughly inoculated with all the microbes they need for fermentation to unfold. So what is the difference between a moldy cabbage and sauerkraut? The curated environment! Lacto-fermentation takes place in an anaerobic (or very-low-oxygen) environment. To set the stage for lacto-fermentation, we submerge our cabbage in liquid, cutting off the air supply for oxygen-loving molds and allowing the lacto-fermenting bacteria to work their magic. Creating an anaerobic environment is the most important condition to curate in this type of fermentation.

Lactic acid–forming bacteria are also more tolerant of higher salt concentrations than most other microbes, and their preferred pH is a bit lower than many of the unwanted microbial varieties as well. We can further tip the scale in their favor by adding salt or by lowering the initial pH with the addition of vinegar, whey, or liquid from another ferment. Neither of these steps is crucial to a robust ferment, and a low-sodium ferment is easily accomplished by skipping the salt addition. For fermenters making salt-free versions, though, we encourage you to acidify your ferment for additional protection until it gets going on its own. Most people who are not on a sodium-restricted diet prefer to add a healthy amount of salt, as it complements the flavor of lacto-fermentation and helps the vegetables retain their crispness.

INGREDIENTS

With lactic acid–forming bacteria already coating their surface, pretty much any raw vegetable will be able to start a fine lacto-ferment, as long as it is not peeled or cooked. Remember, the microbes live on the surface, so if a vegetable has a peel (like a cucumber, for example), that peel must be kept intact to initiate the ferment! If you are using vegetables that have been peeled or cooked, you will need to add lactic acid–forming bacteria from another source to inoculate the ferment. The most common inoculants are whey from dairy ferments such as yogurt, viili, or clabber or the "juice" from another veggie ferment, such as the brine from a previous batch of lacto-pickles or the liquid from finished sauerkraut.

Some companies sell lacto-fermentation starter cultures. We have never had reason to try them so we cannot offer any advice regarding them. If you are interested in investigating, a quick online search will turn up a number of sources.

Once you have your inoculation taken care of by using either a base of raw, unpeeled vegetables or an inoculant, things can get pretty interesting. You can mix in all sorts of ingredients—cooked, peeled, freeze-dried, frozen, dehydrated, and otherwise treated grains, fruits, and beans—resulting in an endless array of textures and flavors. For instance, one of our favorite ingredients to throw into a sauerkraut-like ferment is a cooked starch, such as mashed potatoes or basmati rice. The cooked food is mixed right in with the raw shredded veggies and pressed into the fermentation vessel. Voilà! You will have a soft, sour, and delicious condiment or dressing. If you add some fruit, either fresh or dried, the ferment will not only have sweet and floral notes, but it will also ferment more quickly, due to the availability of simple sugars. Spices, herbs, and even fresh raw meat can be added to lacto-fermenting vegetables for a distinctive delicacy.

We have played around with adding cubes or slices of fresh raw steak or salmon to our veggie ferments. Some people do this because they really enjoy the flavors and textures it creates, while others are looking for ways to preserve meat. We have never found it tasty or useful to ferment meat or fish in this fashion, so this is not something that we do or can claim any expertise about. If you are interested in this practice, a quick Internet search will return reputable online resources that can help you.

There is no limit to what you can throw into a vegetable lacto-ferment, but delicate leaves, like basil and chard, will all but dissolve. Tough leaves, like collard greens, will usually stay just as tough as the day you chopped them. But experiment with small batches. You'll find some unique and personal favorites.

Consider the size of the substrate you ferment. If the ingredient is very firm, like raw butternut squash or carrot, it will take longer for the bacteria to get to the middle and do their work. With these firm foods, smaller pieces work best. For softer ingredients that are easier to penetrate, like sliced cucumbers

and peaches, larger pieces will work better. And if you are using something that has a tough skin, like a whole cucumber, you might puncture the skin with a fork to allow the bacteria to reach the inside a little faster.

That being said, if you do want to ferment, say, a whole uncut cabbage, you can. It will just take a lot longer for the fermentation to progress through the many layers of dense cabbage leaves and then through the core. In the process, the cabbage leaves on the outside will most likely wind up mushy by the time the core begins to soften. It's better to at least quarter the cabbage, or remove the core but keep the leaves whole.

Adding additional sugar sources, like fruits and starchy roots and grains, to your lacto-ferment will accelerate the fermentation time and give you fast, fun results.

SUGGESTIONS FOR ADD-INS TO VEGETABLE FERMENTS:

Wild edible flowers like dandelion or milkweed

Peeled hard-boiled eggs

Raw peeled, cubed, or shredded butternut squash, celeriac, or rutabaga

Cooked and mashed potatoes or sweet potatoes

Seaweed

Cooked grains or beans

Medicinal plants like nettle, chamomile, or ginseng

Raw or toasted cashews, peanuts, almonds, or other nuts

Raw or toasted sesame, mustard, caraway, fennel, coriander, or other seeds

Garlic

Ginger (although too much of this antimicrobial root can slow down some ferments)

Spice mixtures like curry powder, Italian seasoning, or even Mexican seasoning in a fermented salsa

Fresh or dried culinary herbs

For a crispy vegetable ferment that holds up well over time, add some tannins at the beginning of fermentation. Tannins are a polyphenol found in all seeds and wood, in the leaves of a variety of plants, and in the rinds of some fruits. They are most widely known for the texture and flavor they add to wine, but in nature, they slow the onset of degradation in fruits and vegetables. A couple of whole black tea leaves or a pinch of the more commonly found shredded tea added to your vegetable ferment will go a long way in maintaining that crunch they have when just picked. We don't usually lose the crunch in our krauts and kimchi even without added tannins, but we do add tannins to our brine ferments, as the substrate tends toward mushiness otherwise.

Common tannin-containing additions to ferments are whole oak, horseradish, shiso, and grape leaves. Some people use a small piece of dried wood (the size of a dime) or a few fruit stems, like cherry or apple stems, to protect the integrity of their ferment's cell walls. Some variety of black tea is usually on hand in our kitchen, so this is our go-to tannin additive.

While the lactic acid–forming bacteria transform your vegetables, keep in mind that different species of these beneficial microbes are active at different times during the fermentation cycle. In the beginning of a veggie ferment, *Leuconostoc mesenteroides* is the first species to get going. As the activity level of this pioneer species ramps up, the pH drops pretty drastically, bringing the ferment into the range where other lactic acid–forming bacteria like *Lactobacillus plantarum* and *Luteimonas cucumeris* are encouraged to proliferate, and *Leuconostoc mesenteroides* become inactive (although the enzymes they produced continue to function). Once the secondary species have caused the pH to drop even farther, acid-loving species like *Lactobacillus brevis* join the party. The take-home message is that different beneficial bacteria are concentrated at different times during the process, all producing nutrients and enzymes that can do good work inside your gut. It takes about a day for the bacteria to get going in your jar. We encourage you to try eating your fermenting vegetables daily after the first day, to dose yourself with a spectrum of microflora and their nutrients and to experience the fermentation process intimately.

If you want to eat your fermenting veggies daily as the ferment progresses, reach in with a clean fork and gently remove the amount you want from the top. Then slowly press the remaining veggies down beneath the surface of the liquid, being careful not to introduce too much air by rapid mixing or sloshing the fork around. If you do this daily, and gently disturb the entire surface of the liquid, unwanted mold or yeast will never grow because any mold spores trying to get started will be swept under the surface into an anaerobic environment, where they cannot grow.

CURATING THE ENVIRONMENT FOR A DELICIOUS VEGGIE FERMENT

Pay attention to these key factors and your ferments will thrive!

pH

The pH of your ferment can start close to neutral. Some people like to add ingredients to lower the pH somewhat and to introduce more fermenting bacteria, but this is not crucial for a recipe that contains a good amount of salt. However, if you are making a low-sodium ferment, we do recommend acidifying your ferment by adding a tablespoon of whey (the liquid that pools on the surface of yogurt or viili), raw apple cider vinegar, or "juice" from a previous batch of fermented veggies per cup of substrate.

Oxygen

Lactic acid–forming bacteria thrive in anaerobic conditions. For this reason, the ingredients in this style of fermentation are submerged under liquid. This liquid can be water, brine, or the juice squeezed from the veggies themselves. If the surface above the liquid is exposed to oxygen, a yeasty film or mold may develop on the surface. It is generally agreed that this can be carefully scraped from the surface and will not have adverse effects on the ferment's flavor or health attributes. However, some experts disagree, arguing that some molds grow tendrils down into the ferment, leaving an unsavory chemical signature that might affect both quality and flavor. In our home kitchen, we take simple measures to reduce or eliminate the possibility of mold growth. Take a look at Chapter 2: Fermenter's Pantry for ideas and pay attention to the vessels we use in the recipes.

Salt

The desirable lactic acid–forming bacteria are more tolerant of higher salt concentrations than the unwanted, undesirable microbes that can invade a ferment, so we recommend adding salt to lacto-ferments. Additionally, most people prefer the flavor that salt adds to their veggie ferments. For people on a sodium-restricted diet, we recommend acidifying ferments initially, because acidification provides additional protection.

Temperature

Another consideration for lactic acid vegetable ferments is the temperature at which they ferment. Up to a point, the colder the temperature, the slower the ferment, the more balanced the flavor, and the crisper the vegetables. Fermenting in warmer temperatures will result in a quicker final product, more acidic flavors and, depending on the substrate, you may lose some of its crispness. A good temperature to ferment vegetables is 72°F, but the ferment is possible in a wide range, from approximately 40°F to 99°F.

Vessels

We have found it easiest to use Fido-style swing-top jars with rubber gaskets or jars outfitted with air locks for this type of ferment. The seal created by these type of jars will allow the gases building up to escape while preventing oxygen from entering. Veggie ferments are successful in a variety of other vessels, though. When we don't have a swing-top at hand, a simple mason jar with the lid screwed on loosely will do the trick. If you go with a simple mason jar and lid, to prevent mold from growing on the oxygen-rich surface, use a clean fork to disturb the liquid on the surface every couple of days. Any mold spore that tries to set up shop on the surface will be killed when turned into the acidic solution underneath. Ceramic crocks, whether closed-top or open-air, are also popular for this type of ferment. For more about ceramic crocks, other fermentation vessels, and pest control, see Chapter 2: The Fermenter's Pantry.

Long-term storage

When you've tasted your ferment and it has developed the level of acidity and flavor characteristics that you are craving, you can store it indefinitely (for years!) in the fridge or in a cool root cellar. In some societies, people bury fermented foods in the cool earth of their yard. Cooled, the fermentation will continue to progress, but very slowly. Expect the ferment to become more acidic if it is stored for a long period of time, but the acid profile will be mellower, leaning away from vinegary characteristics.

SAUERKRAUT AND BAECHU KIMCHI

Although sauerkraut and baechu kimchi (a type of kimchi that is spicy and cabbage-based) occupy very distinct niches in the culinary world, they are quite similar in style. Both are cabbage-based lactic-acid ferments that do not use the addition of brine or water to create the anaerobic environment. By squeezing and massaging the vegetables, we break down cell walls and release the liquid within. We then pack the wet vegetables and other ingredients into fermentation vessels to create oxygen-free conditions, which this type of ferment thrives in.

Cabbages make a great base for this style of ferment because of their high moisture content and their sweet but slightly bitter flavor. As long as there is enough moisture in the vessel to surround all the pieces and fill all the space between them, pretty much anything can be added, and the adaptations are endless. The three recipes below provide a good starting point for your adventures in this style of brine-free lacto-fermentation. The Basic Sauerkraut recipe is a wetter ferment with liquid levels that will rise high above the cabbage. The Baechu Kimchi recipe is not as wet and relies on a tight packing job of the moist ingredients to create the anaerobic environment your lactic acid–forming bacteria will need. Finally, we share with you our own adaptation of brine-free ferments. The Asian Pear Curried Kimchi is a blend of ideas and preferences that highlight some of the possibilities. Along the way we include some ideas for how to use these ferments in meals throughout the day.

Sauerkraut

Sauerkraut is a staple in our kitchen. We pile it on sandwiches, use it as a salad dressing, cook sausages in it, and eat it by the forkful straight from the jar. Our four-year-old loves it and is guaranteed to get his daily dose of vitamin C if we put out a small bowl of kraut for him as a snack or side dish.

The keys to great sauerkraut are the size of the cabbage pieces and the temperature at which you ferment it. The pieces have to be the right size and the temperature just right to get great texture and acidity at the same time. Long, thin strands are our favorite, and longer, cooler ferments are ideal. If the ambient temperature that your fermenting jar sits in is too high, the cabbage may become softer than desired. In warmer climes, try adding a few leaves of black tea to your ferments; their tannins have a crunch-protecting effect.

Use the Basic Sauerkraut recipe below as a starting point. As mentioned earlier in this chapter, you can add pretty much anything to a veggie lacto-ferment. If you add a sugar or starch, such as fruits, cooked grains, or cooked tubers, the fermentation process will happen faster. After you've tried a few variations, you'll get to know what results you are looking for and can tailor your recipes to your whims.

Some tried-and-true sauerkraut additions include:

Garlic

Caraway seeds

Mustard seeds

Fennel seeds

Turmeric

Shredded apple

Shredded carrot

Raisins

* * * * * * * *

BASIC SAUERKRAUT

Yield: ½ gallon

2 medium heads organic cabbage (about 7 pounds total)

3 tablespoons sea salt

1. Carefully remove 2 to 3 outer leaves of each of the cabbages, keeping the leaves whole. Set the leaves aside.

2. Cut off and discard the exposed stalk. Shred the cabbage finely with a mandoline or slice thinly with a sharp knife.

3. In a large bowl, mix the cabbage and salt together thoroughly. Cover and let sit at room temperature for 10 minutes.

4. After the cabbage has rested with the salt, it will be wet, as the water from the cabbage leaves has migrated toward the salt by osmosis. Aggressively squeeze and massage the cabbage for about 8 minutes to release more of the liquid. Keep massaging the cabbage until a good amount of liquid comes out when you pick up a handful and squeeze it. It should behave as if you were squeezing a wet sponge.

5. Pack the cabbage into the vessels. Start by placing a large handful of wet salted cabbage into the jar. Make a fist and push the cabbage down with the backs of your knuckles. When you push on the cabbage, liquid will gush out of it and start to pool. When the cabbage is compressed as tightly as possible, add more cabbage to the jar and repeat. As you add more and more cabbage, you should be able to push the cabbage farther down below the surface of the pooling liquid. Keep packing until the cabbage is about an inch below the surface of the liquid and there are about 2 inches of headspace above the liquid in your jar.

The headspace will allow for some expansion as the fermentation progresses, and the volume of air will be small enough that the oxygen will quickly be displaced by CO2. If there is liquid left over in the large bowl and your cabbage is not com-

pletely covered, add the remaining liquid. If you do not have enough liquid to thoroughly submerge the cabbage, top it off with drinking water.

6. Spread out the reserved whole cabbage leaves and press them onto the top of the kraut one at a time until they completely cover the surface of the shredded cabbage. You may not need to use all of them; the purpose is to hold down the finely shredded cabbage, keeping it submerged under the surface of the liquid. Make sure the whole leaves are also submerged; push them beneath the surface of the liquid as far as you can. Using a butter knife or chopstick, push the edges of the whole leaves down the sides of the jars to wedge them between the sides and the shredded cabbage that will become your kraut.

7. Close the lid of your vessel and allow the jar to stand at room temperature for 2 to 4 weeks. As the ferment progresses, the production of CO_2 will cause air bubbles to percolate up through the ferment and either be trapped (if your lid is tightly sealed) or it will escape (if using an air lock, a loosely closed lid, or a Fido-style jar with a rubber gasket). If the pressure is allowed to build up, your vessel will likely break, ruining your ferment and making a mess of your kitchen. (For more on appropriate vessels to use to ensure the escape of gases, refer to chapter 2.) As the gases percolate up from the fermenting cabbage, the whole cabbage leaves pressed onto the surface may also be pushed up above the surface of the liquid. If this happens, open the vessel and use a clean fork to push the air out of the leaves and press them back down so they are submerged. We highly recommend sampling some of the sauerkraut along the way, making sure to gently push the cabbage back down beneath the surface of the liquid after you taste it, and then cover the jar again.

8. You decide when your ferment is ready. The sauerkraut is healthful throughout the fermentation process, from day one to day thirty and beyond. When you're happy with the level of acidity and the texture and don't want the kraut to get any more acidic or lose any more crunch, remove the whole cabbage leaves from the surface and store the jar in your refrigerator or root cellar. The flavor and texture will continue to change, albeit very slowly, over time in cold storage.

* * * * * * * *

KRAUT SALT

A fun addition to your spice collection, sauerkraut salt can be used on salads, soups, and anything that needs a little livening up with this salty-sour-earthy flavor. You will need a dehydrator for this recipe. In the absence of a dehydrator, some people use their oven with the

door propped open and set on a very low temperature. There are many tutorials online, if you are interested in trying this method of dehydration.

Yield: 1½ cups

3 cups sauerkraut

½ cup sauerkraut juice or water

1. Place the ingredients in a blender and blend on high until smooth, about 30 seconds.

2. Spread the mixture as uniformly as possible, about ⅛ inch thick, on nonstick dehydrator sheets.

3. Dehydrate at 115°F for 8 hours. The kraut puree will be dry to the touch, but moist like leather when finished.

4. Peel the kraut leather off the dehydrator sheets and put into the dry canister of a powerful blender, such as a Vitamix. Grind at medium speed until fine. Alternatively, use a spice mill or mortar and pestle to grind the salt.

5. Place in a saltshaker along with a teaspoon of rice to absorb moisture. Keeps for 1 month at room temperature or up to 6 months if refrigerated.

* * * * * * * *

KRAUT SALT GOMASIO

To take your kraut salt a step further and create a nutrient-dense, flavorful, low-salt, and high-class culinary seasoning, make this gomasio! You will find endless uses for it, from spicing eggs to topping raw kale salad; you really can't go wrong with this one.

Yield: 2 cups

2 tablespoons Kraut Salt (page 69)

1 tablespoon sea salt

2 cups white or black sesame seeds

½ sheet dried nori (approximately 4 inches x 6 inches)

1. Heat a medium-size frying pan over medium heat. Add sauerkraut salt and sea salt, and stir constantly for about 1 minute. The salts will brown lightly and give off a faint aroma. Pour the salt mixture into a mortar, blender, spice grinder, or small food processor, and set aside.

2. Put sesame seeds into the same warm pan and toast over medium heat, stirring constantly for approximately 4 minutes. The seeds will give off a nice aroma, pop a little bit, and—if they were light-colored seeds—turn a nice golden-brown color when they are done. Add the seeds to the salts.

3. Put the half sheet of nori in the hot pan and toast until crispy and dry, about 45 seconds. Crumble toasted nori into the seed-salt mixture.

4. Pulse the toasted ingredients in the grinder until about half the seeds crack.

5. Store your gomasio in an airtight container in your refrigerator and use within 3 months.

* * * * * * * *

SAUERKRAUT, APPLE, AND FENNEL SALAD WITH WALNUTS

Yield: 4 servings

6 cups lettuce, rinsed and chopped (red leaf lettuce or baby mixed greens work well)

2 cups Basic Sauerkraut (page 67)

1 apple, cored and chopped (sweet varieties such as Cameo, Pink Lady, and Gala work well)

1 fennel bulb, about ½ pound, sliced thin

1 cup chopped walnuts

4 tablespoons extra-virgin olive oil

Salt and pepper

1. Arrange lettuce, sauerkraut, apple pieces, fennel slices, and chopped walnuts in one large serving bowl or separately on 4 salad plates.

2. Drizzle with olive oil. Season with salt and pepper to taste.

Another way to compose a great probiotic-rich side salad is to ferment the apple, fennel, and walnuts with the cabbage. Instead of chopping all the apples, cut some into large rounds and slide them down the edges of a glass fermentation jar with a chopstick or butter knife after it's been packed with the other ingredients so you can admire their beautiful shapes from outside. It will look great on the fermentation shelf. Then, to make a salad, add this finished sauerkraut to the lettuce and proceed with step 2.

Baechu Kimchi

We find kimchi to be one of the most compelling of the veggie ferments. The secret to the almost otherworldly pleasure of kimchi is in the layering of its sensual elements: flavor, texture, aroma, effervescence, heat, salt, umami, acidity, and color. Korean cuisine is a brilliant display of freshness and contrast that is unified by the delicately constructed flavors and varieties of kimchi.

Early kimchi was mainly radish-based and was fermented in a salted stock, paste, or brine. It wasn't until much later that trade brought napa cabbage into the picture, and in the seventeenth century, trade finally brought red peppers to Korea from the Americas and it became an essential ingredient in kimchi. Today, salted and fermented vegetables are considered essential dietary staples all over Asia, where they are believed to aid in the digestibility of grains by stimulating salivation.

Koreans make many varieties of traditional kimchi that are region- and season-dependent. Of the hundreds or perhaps thousands of kimchi styles, most are mildly acidic and gently fizzy. These characteristics are accomplished with a shorter fermentation time at room temperature followed by a longer fermentation at a colder temperature. This combination of temperature conditions encourages microbes that are not very acid-tolerant but that produce high amounts of CO_2 to dominate the profile.

For a more in-depth look at various kimchi styles, check out Lauryn Chun's *The Kimchi Cookbook: 60 Traditional and Modern Ways to Make and Eat Kimchi* or *Kimchi: Essential Recipes of the Korean Kitchen* by Byung-Hi and Byung-Soon Lim.

* * * * * * * *

BAECHU KIMCHI

This recipe will make a complex ferment with delicate layers of flavor that most Westerners will recognize as kimchi and appreciate.

Yield: 1 quart

1 large head napa cabbage (about 2¼ pounds)

1 tablespoon sea salt

⅔ cup gochugaru (Korean chili powder)

⅔ cup chopped scallions

1½ teaspoons minced garlic

2 teaspoons ginger juice (from finely grated ginger squeezed through a cheesecloth)

1 cup grated daikon

2 teaspoons fish sauce

1 tablespoon sugar

1. Separate the cabbage leaves and rinse them well.

2. Cut the leaves in half lengthwise.

3. Place the cabbage in a colander, toss with the sea salt and allow to drain for 45 minutes to 1 hour. Rinse the cabbage leaves well, and spin dry in a salad spinner or pat dry with a kitchen towel or with paper towels.

4. Mix the remaining ingredients in a large bowl until a paste forms. Toss the cabbage leaves in the paste, making sure to coat all the leaves on all sides.

5. One by one, tightly roll up the coated cabbage leaves and place them snugly, side-by-side in layers in a clean 1-quart vessel. Fido-style jars work best for this style of ferment as the seal allows effervescence to build up but not so much that it will cause the jar to break. Unlike the Basic Sauerkraut recipe (page 67) where the cabbage is ultimately submerged underneath the liquid, this kimchi is moist, but not liquid-filled, and relies on a dense packing job to create the anaerobic environment lactic acid–forming bacteria thrive in. Pack the leaves tightly to remove as much air as possible, but don't use a strong level of force, which will destroy the shape and integrity of the leaves. Fill the jar this way leaving 1½ inches of headspace.

6. Close the jar and let rest at room temperature for 24 hours. Place the jar in the refrigerator for 9 days, and then start eating! Kimchi will stay good in the fridge for 6 months or more, and the flavors will continue to mellow and fuse.

SCOBY and starter being added to sweet tea.

Using a sample thief to sample the brew.

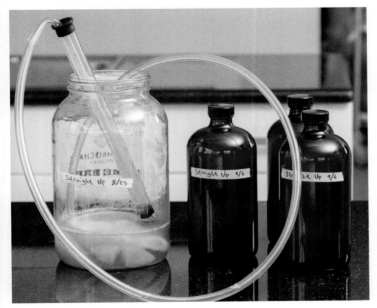

Post-bottling with auto siphon that was used.

Adding sugar to pineapple and spices.

Ingredients in fermentation.

Bottles after 48 hours of bottle conditioning.

Adding beans to water.

Checking the temperature.

TOP LEFT: *Poking holes in fermentation bags.* TOP RIGHT: *Adding starter to cooled beans.*
BOTTOM LEFT: *Filling bags with beans.* BOTTOM RIGHT: *Filled bags left to ferment.*

Equipment and sanitizer ready for home brewing.

TOP LEFT: *Adding grain to make the mash.* TOP RIGHT: *Preparing grain for the sparge.*
BOTTOM LEFT: *Adding hops during the boil.* BOTTOM RIGHT: *Letting the wort cool before adding yeast.*

TOP LEFT: *Activating the yeast.* TOP RIGHT: *Active fermentation with blow-off tube.*
BOTTOM LEFT: *Calm fermentation with air lock.* BOTTOM RIGHT: *Bottling after fermentation.*

Capping a bottle

* * * * * * * *

NOURISHING BREAKFAST BOWL WITH BAECHU KIMCHI

Yield: 1 serving

¼ cup brown rice

1½ cups stock or water

⅛ cup sliced cucumber

⅛ cup sliced carrots

1 scallion, chopped

1 tablespoon miso

⅛ cup Baechu Kimchi (facing page)

1 tablespoon sesame seeds

Tamari, to taste (optional)

1. Rinse rice two or three times or until water runs clear. Put rice and stock or water into a saucepan over high heat, bring to a boil, and then turn down the heat to a low simmer. Cover and let cook until the rice has absorbed most of the liquid, about 35 minutes.

2. Put the rice into a bowl. Arrange vegetables on top.

3. Add a dollop of miso and a small pile of kimchi, and sprinkle with sesame seeds. Season with tamari to taste if desired.

MAKING STOCK

Once we began the practice of making stock in our home, we quickly wondered how we ever got by without it. Simple to make, it has a zillion applications and can transform food into rich, easy to digest, nourishing meals. We braise greens in it, use it for quick sauces and gravies, cook grains and beans in it, add it to sautés, stew meats in it, add it to savory waffles or pancakes, and even use it as a brine for veggie ferments! To make stock, all you need are bones and/or vegetable scraps. Whenever we cook a chicken or bone-in meat, we save the bones and throw them in a pot with vegetable scraps. We always make sure to add onions and/or garlic; other than that, the sky's the limit. Stalks from leafy greens, carrot tops, celery ends, herb stems, corn cobs, bean tips, even leftover chunks of fruit and apple peels or mango skin—all these are fair game. If you use something super flavorful or colorful, like beets, your stock will reflect it; add beets for a red and sweet stock. Some people like to add a small amount of acid, like a tablespoon of vinegar or a squeeze of lemon, to the broth to bring out more of the nutrients. Make a rejuvenating vegan potassium broth using the peels from potatoes or sweet potatoes along with celery parts, carrot parts, and/or parsley parts.

Cover the ingredients with water, and simmer on low heat for up to 24 hours. Even an hour of cooking will result in something useful and yummy, but the longer it cooks, the more nutrients and flavor the stock will take on. Slow cookers come in handy when we cook the stock overnight or have to leave the house. After straining the stock with a fine-mesh strainer, we freeze our stock in a silicone muffin pan so we can use it in small portions.

* * * * * * * *

ASIAN PEAR CURRIED KIMCHI

Yield: 1½ quarts

Somewhere between a kraut and a kimchi, this recipe combines all our favorite veggie ferment characteristics into one jar. The use of napa cabbage, which is quite delicate, along with the strong but floral sweetness of Asian pear, results in a perfect crunch matched by pleasant acidity after a short fermentation cycle of about four days. We also love the soft, creamy consistency of fermented cashews combined with the earthy spice of Indian curry. We throw in seaweed for color, texture, and the added health benefits it brings.

1 large head napa cabbage (3 pounds)

2 tablespoons sea salt

1–2 dried shiitake mushrooms

2 tablespoons dry arame, soaked in cold water until soft, and drained

¾ cup medium-diced Asian pear

1½ tablespoons ginger juice

3 scallions, cut into long slivers

2 cloves garlic, sliced thin

1 teaspoon curry powder

1 cup raw cashews

½ teaspoon chili powder

¼ teaspoon turmeric

1. Separate and rinse the cabbage leaves, and cut them into 2-inch squares. Toss the cabbage with 1 tablespoon of the sea salt, place in a colander, and allow to drain for 45 minutes to 1 hour.

2. While you wait, bring ½ cup water to a boil over high heat. Once boiling, turn off heat source, add the shiitake mushrooms. and the remaining 1 tablespoon sea salt. Cover and allow to steep for 20 minutes. Remove the soaked mushrooms for another use and set aside the mushroom broth.

3. Rinse the cabbage well, and spin dry in a salad spinner or pat dry with kitchen towels or with paper towels. In a large bowl, mix the cabbage with the remaining ingredients and then add ¼ cup of the shiitake mushroom broth.

4. Pack the cabbage mixture into a wide-mouth vessel suitable for anaerobic fermentation. Start by placing one or two large handfuls in the jar, make a fist, and then push the cabbage down with the backs of your knuckles. When the cabbage is well condensed, add some more to the jar and repeat. Keep packing until the liquid is 1½ inches above the surface of the kimchi and there are two inches of headspace in the vessel above the surface. If more liquid is required, add the remaining mushroom broth or drinking water.

5. Cover the jar loosely or seal with an air lock and allow to ferment at room temperature for 3 days. The ferment is rather quick because of the availability of simple sugars.

6. Place the kimchi in the refrigerator. It will keep for at least 6 months in the fridge and the flavors will continue to mellow in storage. Enjoy!

Our evolutionary ancestors came from the sea and crawled out to become land mammals. Then some of those mammals dived back into the sea and became whales, dolphins, and sea lions. The rest of us stayed land-bound and continued evolving into bipeds and eventually humans. The sea remains a wealth of nutritional resources for us, even though we left our aquatic past behind us.

Seaweed is rich in essential nutrients such as iodine and potassium. It is an extraordinarily rich source of antioxidants and helps subdue inflammation. Research has suggested that seaweed helps regulate hormones in the body as well.

Regardless of the health benefits, we love the tastes, flavors, and textures that seaweed imparts. We toss large pieces of dried kelp into soups, grains, and beans while they are cooking and either remove them or slice them up to serve as a garnish. It is also nice to toss all forms of smaller seaweeds, like wakame and arame, into dishes and ferments.

BRINE-FERMENTED VEGGIES

Brine fermentation is useful for fermenting whole vegetables and larger vegetable chunks like pickles and giardiniera. The basic principles of this style of fermentation are the same as in the brineless recipes above. Both are lacto-fermentations that are carried out under anaerobic conditions and are more tolerant of higher salt and lower pH levels. In brine fermentation, whole vegetables or chunks of veggies are submerged in a liquid. Usually this liquid is salty, but it does not have to be. If you go the sodium-free route, we suggest that you add some acidifying agent initially to protect your ferment from unwanted microbial growth. We like to use whey or the juice from a previous ferment to both acidify and add additional lactic acid–forming bacteria to the pot.

Brine recipes are based on an approximate ratio of salt to water of about two tablespoons salt per quart of water. From there, the sky is the limit—you can add a wide variety of flavor-enhancing ingredients. Some of our favorite brine additions are the standard dill and garlic. You can add lemon zest, orange slices, peppercorns, mustard seeds, brown sugar, maple syrup, rosemary, thyme, oregano, hot peppers, sweet peppers, and any number of spices, fruits, and flavors to your brine. In addition, when setting up a brine ferment, we always add some form of tannin to keep our veggies crisp (see page 63).

What can you brine? Pretty much any firm vegetable or fruit can be fermented: carrots, cucumbers, cauliflower, peppers, string beans, snow peas, onions, lemons, oranges, beets, summer squash, scallions, fennel, asparagus, and the list goes on and on. Even vegetables that would ordinarily be cooked, like butternut squash, sweet potatoes, rhubarb, and okra, can be eaten raw when fermented. Refer back to the beginning of chapter 3 for a more thorough list of ingredients to add to any veggie ferments. And remember, if you begin with only vegetables or fruits that are cooked or peeled, they will not have the lactic acid–forming bacteria intact to inoculate your ferment. You will need to add an inoculant, such as whey or juice from another ferment.

Bread-and-butter pickles are a symphony of sweet and sour that use a combination of common ingredients: Vidalia onion, celery leaves, red pepper flakes, fenugreek, fennel seeds, turmeric, mustard seeds, allspice, cloves, bell peppers, cider vinegar, maple syrup, molasses, and brown sugar.

BASIC BRINE

Use this recipe as a base for any brine ferment. You can switch out the spices and herbs but leave the salt ratio intact. If you are making a no-salt batch, replace the salt with an equal volume of whey or juice from a previous ferment as added protection against contamination. Just mix up the brine, wedge the veggies you wish to ferment in the brine in order to keep them submerged under the liquid, and allow to stand at room temperature for seven to fourteen days or until the level of acidity you are going for is reached. For an example of a delicious mix using this recipe, check out Lacto-Fermented Giardiniera.

Yield: Enough brine for a 1-quart ferment

1 scallion

3 cloves garlic, peeled and crushed

1 5-inch frond dill

2 bay leaves

2 whole black tea leaves, grape leaves, or oak leaves

1 teaspoon mustard seeds

1½ tablespoons sea salt

3 cups water

LACTO—FERMENTED GIARDINIERA

Yield: 1 quart

1 medium head cauliflower (about 2 pounds)

4 large carrots (about 1 pound)

2 red peppers (about ½ pound)

1 recipe Basic Brine

1. Cut the cauliflower into 1-inch chunks, slice the carrots into ¼-inch rounds, and slice the red peppers into ¼-inch slices.

2. Put the vegetables into a 1-quart vessel appropriate for anaerobic fermentation. Arrange them in tight layers so that they will hold themselves in place below the surface of the brine, once it is added in the next step.

3. Pour the brine over the vegetables, herbs, and spices, making sure all solids are completely submerged underneath the liquids.

4. Close the lid and allow to sit at room temperature for 5 to 7 days, or until the desired acidity is reached. When your brine-fermented veggies are ready, move them to the fridge, where they will keep for 3 months or more, depending on the type of vegetable. Some vegetables will get softer in the fridge more rapidly than others. Experiment with

your particular vegetable choices. In general the firmer the vegetable to start with, the better it holds up. When you notice your veggies are getting softer, go ahead and use them up in a creative recipe and start a new batch.

* * * * * * * *

SOY SAUCE—BRINED JAPANESE PICKLES

Yield: 1 pint

2–3 pickling cucumbers (approximately ½ pound)

2–3 cloves garlic, peeled and chopped

1-inch piece of ginger, peeled and chopped

¼ cup quality soy sauce (shoyu or tamari)

1–2 teaspoons toasted sesame oil

1. Thinly slice the pickling cucumbers.

2. Tightly pack the cucumbers, garlic, and ginger into a pint-size vessel appropriate for anaerobic fermentation, so that they all hold each another down.

3. Pour the soy sauce into the jar, adding more if necessary to completely submerge all the ingredients, and secure the lid on the jar loosely or outfit with an air lock or another gas-release closure.

4. Allow to ferment at room temperature for 3 to 7 days. Add the toasted sesame oil and store in the refrigerator, where it will keep for 6 months.

LACTO-FERMENTED CONDIMENTS

A cornucopia of delicious condiments can be perfected in a fermentation vessel. The salty, acidic flavor profile characteristic of lacto-ferments is the ideal enhancement alongside a wide variety of dishes.

In contrast to the recipes for sauerkraut or brine-ferments, which use the microbial profile of raw vegetable skins to inoculate the ferment, the following recipes rely on the addition of a starter to inoculate the substrate with the culture of lactic acid–forming microbes that will ferment the condiment.

Sources of lacto-ferment starter cultures are:

Whey from yogurt, viili, or clabber

Brine from previous veggie ferments

Beet or bread kvass

* * * * * * * *

FERMENTED KETCHUP

Yield: 2 cups

¼ cup maple syrup

2 cups tomato paste

¼ cup plus 2 tablespoons fresh whey, kombucha, or veggie ferment juice

2 tablespoons raw apple cider vinegar plus additional as needed

1 teaspoon unrefined sea salt

1 teaspoon allspice

¼ teaspoon ground cloves

1. In a medium bowl, add the maple syrup and the tomato paste, and fold together. Whisk in ¼ cup of the whey, kombucha, or veggie ferment juice, the apple cider vinegar, the sea salt, and the spices. Mix well, until uniform.

2. Spoon the homemade ketchup into a clean mason jar, and top with the remaining 2 tablespoons fresh whey, kombucha, or veggie ferment juice. Cover tightly with a lid.

3. Allow the mixture to sit at room temperature, undisturbed, for 3 to 5 days. When it has fermented to your liking, stir, thin with apple cider vinegar if needed, and refrigerate. The ketchup will keep, in refrigeration, for several months.

* * * * * * * *

SPICY HONEY DILL MUSTARD

This mustard will quickly become a staple in your kitchen, as it has in ours. We use it to dress fantastic croque monsieurs, dip bangers in, and smother our salmon fillets in before searing them at a high temperature. The possibilities here are endless, as long as they require a bit of heat and a lot of flavor! We even dip into the seeds while they are fermenting on the counter to add some zing to eggs, soups, and greens. Just remember, if you steal some from the fermentation jar, when you blend them with the dill and honey, you'll have to adjust the recipe.

Yield: 1 cup

½ cup whole brown mustard seeds

1½ cup very acidic kombucha (can substitute raw apple cider vinegar)

¼ cup chopped fresh dill

¼ teaspoon sea salt

3 tablespoons honey

1. Mix mustard seeds and 1¼ cup of kombucha in a small jar, making sure there is at least ¼ inch of liquid above the seeds. Add more kombucha if necessary.

2. Loosely cover the jar with the lid and allow to ferment at room temperature for at least 3 days and up to 2 weeks. Keep the jar somewhere conspicuous and take a look at it often to make sure the seeds are not poking out of the liquid. If they are, add more kombucha to keep them submerged.

3. Pour the fermented mixture into a blender. Add the remaining ¼ cup of kombucha and the dill, sea salt, and honey. You can either pulse the mixture until the desired coarse-grind is reached or, for a smoother consistency, puree periodically, stopping to scrape the sides with a spatula. If you are aiming for a smooth consistency, you may wish to add more kombucha along the way.

4. When the desired consistency is reached, place your mustard in a sealable container and refrigerate. It will keep for 6 months or more.

* * * * * * * *

RHUBARB CHUTNEY

Yield: 1 pint

3 stalks rhubarb, trimmed of any ends and leafy green portions

½ cup dried figs

¼ cup chopped raw pistachios

½ teaspoon sea salt

¼ cup whey or sauerkraut juice

½ teaspoon ground cinnamon

About ⅓ cup water

1. Coarsely chop the rhubarb, figs, and pistachios. In a medium bowl, mix the chopped fruit and nuts with the salt, whey or sauerkraut juice, and cinnamon. Add about ⅓ cup water to make a chutney consistency.

2. Spoon into a quart-size vessel appropriate for anaerobic fermentation. Push the chunky parts down below the surface of the liquid, and close. Allow to ferment at room temperature. You should see the mixture bubbling. If need be, push the fruits and nuts down periodically so they remain submerged in the liquid.

3. Taste the chutney after 2 days. Ferment for up to 4 days—at 4 days the mixture will have lost a lot of its sweetness and will have a bright zesty taste, and possibly some effervescence.

4. Cover tightly, and store in the fridge for up to 3 weeks. Serve with meats, curries, on sandwiches and more! It is especially delightful alongside the Idli recipe (page 113)

chapter 4

∽ DAIRY LACTO–FERMENTATION ∾

For as long as large mammals have been domesticated, humans have consumed fermented milk. Similar to raw vegetables, raw milk is home to indigenous lacto-fermenting bacteria that not only preserve the milk from unwanted spoilage but also bestow interesting changes to the liquid, and they do it pretty quickly. Before the advent of pasteurization and refrigeration—which, respectively, kills the indigenous culture and slows down the fermentation process—all milk that was consumed was fermented to some degree.. The moment fresh raw milk is collected, the fermentation process begins.

Humans have also long been adding outside microbial cultures to milk. For example, before lightweight alternatives were developed, the skins and inner membranes of animals were traditionally used to carry around foods and beverages. Such animal materials came inoculated with their own resident microbial populations. *Airag*, a Mongolian milk ferment, is a great example of how complex and unique milk ferments evolved in ancient cultures (see sidebar). Similar in origin, most cheeses are coagulated using rennet, enzymes harvested from the stomachs of ruminants.

* * * * * * * *

Imagine a Mongolian herder who carries refreshment in an animal bladder when she sets out for a few days on the plains with her charges for overnight stays in the fields. She fills the animal bladder with some fresh raw milk from one of her village's breeding horses and heads out on foot. As the milk sloshes inside the bladder to the rhythm of her walk, the microbial population from the lining of the bladder mingle with the indigenous milk cultures, and a new ferment is underway! The next day, the milk is a thicker, mildly acidic, bubbly, and slightly alcoholic beverage. Delicious, refreshing, and easy to digest, *airag*, aka *kumis* in other cultures, has higher levels of alcohol than common, modern yogurt because higher levels of sugar are present in mares' milk than in cow's milk and because oxygen-rich conditions are curated in its production. Throughout the Mongol Empire, this relative of modern yogurt was a dietary staple and it spread throughout the Central Asian steppes, where it remains vital today.

* * * * * * * *

Each human community that relied on large domesticated animals had its own practices for handling milk and its own distinct native microbial populations, which resulted in biologically different dairy ferments. Some of those life-sustaining dairy foods died off as these communities were absorbed by modernization. But others have held on, changing hands and crossing seas, and still have a place in the modern home kitchen.

Today, popular milk ferments include yogurts and cheeses, as well as sour cream. In our home fermenting kitchen, we have found that by keeping one culture of viili and a raw milk clabber going all the time, we can meet all our dairy needs . . . and then some. Viili and raw milk clabber can be used to make everything from sour cream to fresh cheeses. They can also be enjoyed like yogurt and used in its place in any recipe. Both viili and clabber are simple to make: the setup for either one takes under a minute, and they ferment quickly, so require little thought. We also make dairy kefir from time to time, as we enjoy its effervescence and slight headiness; this milk ferment is covered in Part III: Drinks.

CHOOSING MILK

The flavor, consistency, and longevity of your dairy culture are determined, in part, by the milk you choose. You should consider the milk's pasteurization, type, fat content, homogenization, and origin when deciding which milk to work with.

Pasteurization

Steer clear of ultrapasteurized milk, which has been heated to a higher temperature than pasteurized milk. This changes the chemical composition of the milk and results in a ferment that does not coagulate. Although raw milk can be cultured with non-native microbes, keep in mind that it comes along with its own native culture that will compete with any community you introduce. If you are fermenting yogurt or viili using raw milk, the ferment will include the native microbes in addition to the ones you introduce and the qualities (flavor, consistency, time to completion, etc) will be altered. We have used raw milk to ferment yogurt, viili, and kefir, resulting in wonderfully delicious ferments, but they were not the same as what we get when we pasteurize the milk first. To pasteurize any raw milk, bring it to a barely detectable boil over medium-low heat and simmer for about 30 seconds, stirring constantly. If you have a thermometer handy, you are looking to bring cow's milk to 180°F and other animal-based milks to about 165°F. Be sure to cool down the milk to the right fermentation temperature before adding your culture. Read the recipes to find out more about this.

Milk type

Sheep's milk, goat's milk, or cow's milk will work fine with most dairy ferments. Each type of milk has its own distinct flavor and nutritional profile. Cow's milk is the most easy to come by, followed by goat's milk, then sheep's milk. Other mammalian milks (mare, camel, buffalo, etc) are rare and hard to find. The recipes that follow are compiled for cow's milk, which contains a unique protein whose structure denatures at 180°F. This denaturing allows the protein to bind to other proteins, ostensibly resulting in a firmer, thicker curd. This step is not necessary, and depending on the fat content, pasteurization technique, and culture that you use, this denaturing step can have anywhere from significant to negligible effects.

If you are interested in culturing nondairy milk (such as nut, grain, legume, or seed milk) with bacteria traditionally cultured in dairy products, it is doable, but dairy cultures are typically not well suited for nondairy environments. The fermentation process will likely take longer and the culture will not continue for more than one or two generations. Keep a separate culture fed with dairy as backup. We also recommend using heirloom cultures for nondairy milk; their more stable nature allows them to jump substrates more readily than the laboratory varieties. This is discussed in greater detail in the section "Yogurt," page 85.

Fat content

The fat content of the milk you choose will have a significant effect on the overall result of the ferment. In our home, we don't prefer one fat content over the other, as they each have unique qualities. Lower-fat milk sets and acidifies more quickly, but the coagulated proteins fall apart more easily when stirred. High-fat milks result in silkier foods and beverages that take a little longer to ferment and hold their firmness better when stirred. We tend to feed the kids higher-fat milks, as this nutrient is so essential to healthy development.

Homogenization

Homogenization is essentially the rapid shaking or slamming of the big spheres of fat that would float to the top of whole cow's milk and form the cream. As a result of homogenization, these spheres break up into smaller bits and dissolve more thoroughly throughout the milk. If you use unhomogenized milk in a dairy ferment, you will wind up with two distinctly yummy layers: a thin layer of fermented cream sitting on top of the firm and satiny fermented milk. If you use homogenized milk, the two layers will be integrated and indistinguishable. Both homogenized and unhomogenized milk produce great ferments. Goat's and sheep's milk do not have these large fat spheres and come straight from the animal as a homogenous mix.

Origin: organic, grass-fed versus CAFO

As with all foods and ferments, the quality of your ingredients will determine the quality of your final product. Always begin with the freshest ingredients that you can afford or access. When it comes to milk and all animal products, it is vital that you seek out farms that raise animals humanely—without the use of unnecessary hormones and antibiotics—and that feed the animals as close to their natural diet as possible. Both the meat and the milk produced by pasture-raised animals have far superior nutritive and energetic qualities compared to their industrially produced counterparts.

YOGURT

The word *yogurt* comes from the lexicon of early Central Asian Turks and relates to the word *yoğurmak*, meaning to curdle, coagulate, or thicken. The Central Asian Turks were the first to domesticate one lineage of cattle, the taurine line; another cattle lineage, the indicine line, was domesticated in India. Both civilizations made naturally coagulated and acidified milk ferments, but the Turkish word took root and was passed down through generations to arrive on the grocery lists of Western shoppers.

The main microbial species in today's yogurt are *Lactobacillus delbrueckii* subsp. *bulgaricus* and/or *L. acidophilus* and *Streptococcus salivarius* subsp. *thermophilus*. Several other species can be found in yogurt cultures as well. To make yogurt, you need a yogurt culture, some milk, and an environment suitable for the thermophilic bacteria in the culture. The yogurt culture could be as simple as a dollop of store-bought yogurt that has live bacteria intact (check the label). However, if you use a store-bought variety, chances are you will be able to culture more yogurt only for one or two generations. The cultures used to make commercial yogurts are, by and large, just a few strains that are cultivated in labs; as such, they do not form a whole, sustainable colony that will produce consistent results in perpetuity.

There are several companies that sell actual yogurt starter cultures and you will find them in well-stocked health food stores and online. Most of these commercially available cultures are just like commercially produced live-culture yogurt: they will need to be replaced after just a few generations. You will know that your culture is no longer robust when the yogurt does not set as tightly as it did during the first round of fermentation.

The alternative to a store-bought culture is an heirloom culture that contains not only the above-mentioned species, but also a host of others. These species naturally stabilize the community and provide all the necessary pieces to continue fermenting indefinitely, generation after generation. We have seen one or two cultures on the market that claim to be heirloom varieties, but we have not purchased or tried them. The only way we know of to obtain a reliable heirloom culture is to find another home fermenter who has one. There are various fermenting forums online, where you may be able to connect with someone who has an heirloom culture.

To make yogurt at home, you will usually begin by heating milk up to a slow bubble at 180°F. This denatures, or unwinds, some of the native proteins in the milk and prepares them to be wound up in a different orientation by lacto-fermenting bacteria—which sets yogurt and gives it the smooth, thickened texture we all know and love to slurp. You can just as easily skip this step. Your result will be every bit as delicious, and the texture will be slightly less smooth. Whether or not you choose to denature these proteins, do not add your yogurt culture to milk that is above 110°F. It will kill the culture.

We have found that both skim and low-fat milk produce a firmer yogurt than whole milk, which has a softer, richer consistency. Skim and low-fat milk also tend to ferment a little faster than full-fat milk.

* * * * * * * *

YOGURT

Some people prefer to add thickeners to their yogurt prior to fermentation. In our trials at home, we have found that thickeners make full-fat milk yogurt slightly smoother, but they have little effect on lower-fat and skim milk ferments. When yogurt made without thickeners is put into the blender, it loses its form and liquefies again. We suspect that commercial producers add thickeners to all varieties of commercially produced yogurt to aid in retaining its form through the hustle and bustle of shipment. If you are interested in using thickeners, agar and gelatin are commonly added to the milk prior to fermentation for this purpose.

Yield: 1 quart

1 quart milk (see page 83 for discussion about choosing milk)

2 teaspoons live-culture yogurt

1. Heat the milk in a saucepan over medium heat stirring constantly. If a skin forms on the surface, skim it off and discard it. After a few minutes, the milk will start to lightly bubble at the edge of the pot. If you have a thermometer, it will read close to 180°F— the temperature that denatures the proteins

and prepares them for coagulating nicely. Be careful that you don't allow the milk to get any hotter. You do not want it to boil or scald. Once the light bubbling at the edge is achieved, remove the pot from heat.

2. Cool the milk to 110°F or cooler by setting it aside, covered, or by placing it in an ice bath. Pour the milk into a clean 1-quart glass jar. Stir in the yogurt and screw the lid on loosely to allow gases to escape and to avoid building up pressure in the vessel. Let the fermenting yogurt stand at 110°F for 10 hours. At this point if you gently rock the jar, you should notice that the milk no longer sloshes like a liquid, but is thick and separates from the edges of the jar. The aroma of the milk will be sour but fresh. Your homemade yogurt will keep for 3 weeks in the fridge, during which time the whey will pool on the surface and the yogurt will slowly continue to get more acidic. You can stir the protein-rich whey back into the yogurt or use it to inoculate another lactic-acid forming ferment, like pickles or Fermented Ketchup.

Like many other ferments, yogurt fermented at slightly higher temperatures will yield a more acidic flavor profile while dropping down a couple of degrees will result in mellower flavors. For tips on how to acheive a specific incubation temperature for yogurt, refer to Chapter 2: The Fermenter's Pantry.

---

* * * * * * * *

YOGURT HERB DRESSING

A colorful crudité set out on the table before dinner, when everyone is cycling through the kitchen looking for a quick bite, is a great way to increase your family's daily veggie count. Pair it with this fresh yogurt herb dressing for dipping and your veggies become a nourishing probiotic pre-dinner treat! This dressing also goes great on salads and can even be used to complete potato salads, pasta salads, and sandwiches!

Yield: 2¼ cup

2 cups yogurt

1 tablespoon lemon juice

2 cloves garlic

⅛ teaspoon salt

2 tablespoons extra-virgin olive oil (optional)

¼ cup chopped herbs (parsley, dill, basil, chives, watercress, cilantro, etc.)

1. Put ¼ cup of the yogurt, lemon juice, garlic, salt, and extra-virgin olive oil (if the yogurt is skim or low-fat) in a blender. Blend on high until smooth, then pour into a jar or bottle with a tightly closing top.

2. Add the remaining ¾ cup yogurt and the chopped herbs and close the lid tightly. Shake vigorously. The dressing will keep in the refrigerator for 2 weeks.

* * * * * * * *

YOGURT CHEESE

For fun yogurt cheeses worthy of the fanciest of cheeseboards, mix in finely chopped herbs, spices, hot peppers, veggies, or fruit or swirl in a spoonful of jelly or chutney before letting the yogurt drain overnight. One of our favorite additions is finely chopped chives.

Yield: 2 cups

1 quart plain yogurt

1. Line a colander or fine-mesh strainer with 4 layers of cheesecloth , leaving a few inches of cloth hanging over the edges, and place over a medium bowl.

2. Mix in any additions, then pour the yogurt into cheesecloth-lined colander, cover with a plate or foil, and transfer to the refrigerator. Let it drain for 8 to 12 hours, depending on how firm you would like the cheese. The longer you leave it, the firmer and less watery the cheese will become.

3. Once the cheese has reached the desired consistency, gather the edges of the cheesecloth and transfer the bundle to a plate. Cover the top of cheese with the gathered edges of the cheesecloth and place another plate on top. Press down for about 15 seconds to remove even more of the whey. This results in a drier cheese consistency and more whey to use in other recipes. Your cheese will keep for 1 week in the fridge and longer if you don't use add-ins.

The liquid that comes out during the draining step is called *whey*. Rich with protein, vitamins, and minerals, whey is consumed by many as a health tonic and as a nutrient-dense addition to other recipes, such as smoothies, and marinades, or use it as a milk replacement in baking. Whey has been shown to increase insulin production and aid in blood sugar regulation; however, if you are sensitive to large quantities of lactose, you won't want to consume whey, as the lactose that remains after fermentation has been halted concentrates in the whey.

WAYS TO USE WHEY:

For a refreshing beverage, mix whey with soda water and honey.

To make a nutrient-dense Arnold Palmer, mix whey with tea.

Add whey to new ferments to acidify them and increase their lacto-bacteria count.

Add it instead of water or stock in savory recipes or baking for a mild sourdough flavor.

Reconstitute mushrooms, seaweed, and dried fruits in it.

Use it to thin dips and sauces, such as hummus or pesto.

Use it as a conditioner after shampooing for luxuriously silky hair.

VIILI

Viili (or villi) is another cultured milk in the canon. Originating in Nordic countries, viili is exceptionally easy to make and perpetuate once you have the culture. Its luscious stringiness and mild flavor are exquisite. Like kefir and kombucha, viili is the result of a community made up of yeast and bacteria. But, unique to viili, this community also contains a mold, *Geotrichum candidum*, the labors of which impart a characteristically velvety surface to the ferment. Not coincidentally, this same mold is found on European soft cheeses such as Camembert and is responsible for the cheeses' soft, velvety rind.

Viili is an exquisite ferment, and if you are a dairy eater, we highly recommend you start making it at once. There are a variety of sources for buying viili cultures; the online sites GEM Cultures and Cultures for Health both carry them. Some viili cultures are advertised to not contain *Geotrichum candidum*, but we have not tried them.

Full-fat milk results in a stringier and looser viili. Skim milk won't string when lifted from the pot and holds its shape better. Both are exquisite.

* * * * * * * *

VIILI

Yield: 1 pint

2 tablespoons viili culture

1 pint pasteurized milk, cool or at room temperature

1. Put viili in a 1-pint jar. Roll the jar around to coat its sides and bottom with the viili.

2. Pour in the milk.

3. Cover the jar with a lid and leave at room temperature for 24 hours. When finished, the viili should be dense and coagulated, smell sour, and have a silky texture.

This recipe is easily scalable. We make it in half-gallon jars. Use enough already fermented viili in the beginning to coat the sides of the jar, about ¾ cup if making a half-gallon. Then fill the jar with pasteurized milk.

VIILI SOUR CREAM

Yield: 1 cup

1 pint viili

1 teaspoon lemon juice

1. Line a colander or fine-mesh strainer with 4 layers of cheesecloth, and place over a medium bowl.

2. In a small bowl, mix the viili and the lemon juice. Pour the mixture into the cheesecloth-lined colander. Cover with a small plate and transfer to the refrigerator; allow to drain for 8 hours. The whey will collect in the bowl below and the smooth, thick viili sour cream will be left behind in the cheesecloth.

3. Put viili sour cream in a sealable container. It will keep in the refrigerator for 2 to 3 weeks.

VIILI CHIA BREAKFAST BOWL

Yield: 1 serving

1 cup viili (page 89)

3 tablespoons chia gel (see sidebar)

¼ cup diced fruit, such as bananas, mango, or berries

1 tablespoon maple syrup (optional)

1. Spoon viili into a breakfast bowl and mix in the chia gel.

2. Arrange diced fruit on top.

3. Swirl in the maple syrup and enjoy!

We love chia in our house. It is hydrating and nourishing, adding high-quality fiber, protein, and antioxidants to our diet in a fun and easy way. A jar of chia gel is always waiting in our refrigerator to be added to all sorts of foods. From waffles and eggs to kombucha and simple drinking water, chia gel has many uses. Make chia gel by mixing 2 tablespoons chia seeds and 1 cup water in a sealable jar. Shake 2 to 3 times during the first 10 minutes of soaking, otherwise the seeds will clump. After that, the gel is ready to use. It will keep in refrigeration for one week.

CLABBERED MILK, CURDS, AND WHEY

If left alone at room temperature for a few days, the lactic acid–forming bacteria in raw milk will acidify the milk, causing the proteins to coagulate and the liquid to become thick. The first stage of this ferment is called *clabber*. If the clabber is left to ferment a little bit longer, it will separate into curds and whey (the stuff Little Miss Muffet grew up on). The curds can be drained of any remaining whey to make velvety-rich and nutrient-dense curd cheese, a wonderful substitute for sour cream or cream cheese. The leftover whey is water that is infused with protein, vitamins, and other nutrients.

Now rewind to the clabbered milk stage, and add a dollop of that to fresh raw milk. This time the milk clabbers faster, perhaps taking 36 hours. Take some of this new generation and add it to fresh raw milk a couple more times, and you will arrive at a culture that clabbers milk in about 24 hours. This is buttermilk, which can be perpetuated indefinitely.

* * * * * * * *

CLABBER, BUTTERMILK, CURDS, AND WHEY

You can use buttermilk in recipes for pancakes, muffins, and biscuits and as a replacement for milk in almost any recipe. Save the whey for other uses such as baking or smoothies. The curds can be eaten as-is or they can be strained further with cheesecloth in a colander (see Yogurt Cheese recipe (page 88)) for a firmer consistency.

Yield: 1 pint buttermilk or 1 cup curds and 1 cup whey

1 pint unhomogenized raw milk

1. Pour raw milk into a clean 1-pint jar. Cover loosely with a lid and let sit at room temperature for 3 to 4 days. When it smells slightly acidic and is slightly thicker, it is buttermilk. You may also notice the color has become more yellow. If you refrigerate it now, your buttermilk will keep in the fridge for 2 weeks.

2. Let stand an additional 2 to 4 days, and thick curds will separate out and float in the translucent liquid of whey. Use a cheesecloth-lined colander to strain the curds from the whey in the refrigerator. The longer you leave your curds straining, the drier and more firm they will become—up to 24 hours. Store them both in the refrigerator. They will stay fresh in there for a week.

chapter 5

∽ BEANS AND GRAINS ∽

Here's the paradox: The majority of the world gets its nutrition from beans and grains. Beans and grains are specifically made to withstand digestion.

Beans and grains are seeds. If you plant the wheat berries you buy from the bulk section of your grocery store, you will grow—that's right—wheat! Likewise, your dried lentils, black beans, and chickpeas are seeds and will sprout as well. One of the ways plants go forth and prosper is to have their seeds eaten by birds or beasts and carried to far-off lands, where they are then, ahem, deposited. Seeds use several mechanisms to protect themselves from being digested along the way. First, there is the mechanical. Seeds have a tough, fibrous outer layer called a hull, husk, bran, or seed coat. This armor can range from thin and flimsy to thick and impenetrable. In general, cooking the bean or grain softens the outer layer of even the most tough-hulled seeds and renders them edible. The seed coats of beans and grains contain some protein, some vitamins and minerals, and a lot of fiber, but they are also notoriously difficult to digest, even after cooking.

The second line of defense against digestion is chemical. Phytic acid, one of these defense chemicals, is an antinutrient, which means that it interferes with the body's ability to absorb nutrients. In the seeds of plants, phytic acid holds on tightly to important minerals like calcium, iron, zinc, and phosphorous and vitamins like vitamin B_3. While the seeds move through your body, the phytic acid keeps those nutrients locked up in little molecular cages that your body cannot break into in any amount that would be nutritionally meaningful. For people with largely grain- and bean-based diets, phytic acid contributes to deficiencies in these important nutrients and vitamins.

Another point of consideration is that beans and grains contain oligosaccharides, large molecular complexes of sugar. These compounds are easily broken down by microbes, but the human body lacks the enzyme to properly handle these. The result is that when you consume them, the microbes that inhabit your gut go to work breaking them down (fermenting them!) inside you and the result is a buildup of gases in the GI tract causing cramping and flatulence.

Fermentation harnesses the fantastic powers of microbes to mitigate all three of these problems. Fermenting microbes produce enzymes that break down the fibers in the hulls. They also produce phytase, which annihilates phytic acid. Fermenting microbes also make short work of oligosaccharides before they enter your body, reducing the creation of gases that become uncomfortable when they build up in your GI tract. By fermenting your beans and grains before consuming them, not only will you create conditions that allow your body to break them down more easily (and less painfully), but you will reap the reward of the vitamins and minerals that microbes free from their molecular cages.

> Tofu is not a fermented food, although most consider it a healthful part of Asian cuisine. Through the multistep process of tofu-making, the deleterious compounds in soybeans are ameliorated, making tofu an acceptable dietary addition in reasonable quantities.

MISO

Most people are familiar with miso from Japanese restaurants, where it is mixed with a flavorful broth to make miso soup. Beyond that, miso unfortunately does not occupy much space on the Western plate. In our home, we always have miso on hand and eat it on a daily basis. We highly encourage you to do the same. We use it in our Nourishing Breakfast Bowl with Baechu Kimchi

(page 72), smear it on crackers or rice cakes for a snack, mix it into salad dressings, and smother fish or chicken with it before pan-searing or roasting. Fresh, homemade miso is so versatile and adds a complex, salty, and rich characteristic. And we feel so nourished when we eat it.

Fresh homemade miso is far superior to most of the miso you will find on store shelves. It can be made using any legume. A number of delicious additions can also be incorporated to increase the flavor potential as well as the nutritional profile. Grains, seaweed, and shredded or chopped vegetables are all things we like to incorporate into the bean mash before allowing it to ferment. We always keep the volume of beans greater than the volume of grains, and the volume of the other additions less than 10 percent of the overall mixture. When adding watery vegetables, like reconstituted seaweed, we reduce the amount of liquid in the recipe.

> Our favorite miso flavor combination is a strong leafy green, such as dandelion or mibuna, along with an aromatic, like garlic, leek, scallion, or onion. The final product is nourishing, packed full of healthy plant compounds, and delicious!

Miso fermentation is a two-step process. First, a grain, such as rice or barley, or a bean, such as soy, is inoculated with the mold *Aspergillus oryzae* or another fungal species to make koji. This step is essential to miso fermentation, as the mold gives off certain enzymes and other chemical compounds that help to break down the substrate in the second step. Although koji is apparently easy to make, and those who make it celebrate the process and the aroma it gives off, we have never made it ourselves. Koji is very easy to obtain from a number of sources including GEM Cultures and South River Miso; both can be found on the Internet. Koji is also available in well-stocked grocery stores and Japanese food markets.

* * * * * * * *

If you are interested in making your own koji, GEM Cultures sells several varieties of starter kits that come with detailed instructions on how to make koji at home.

* * * * * * * *

In addition to koji, you will also need some seed miso to start your ferment. To get started, you can buy raw miso from the grocery store to use as seed; later, use miso from a previous batch. GEM Cultures, as well as a few other websites, sells seed miso online.

Traditionally, certain kojis were mixed with certain legumes and, perhaps, grains, then inoculated with specific seed misos and incubated for certain lengths of time. I have found that using any koji with any legume and any seed miso results in good miso. If you wish to ferment for a short period of time, as in the Sweet White Miso recipe below, you will want to use a larger proportion of koji. If you are making a long-fermenting, dark miso like hatcho miso, you will use less koji.

* * * * * * * *

SWEET WHITE MISO

Yield: 4–5 pints

Glass jars with screw-top lids are used here, but this recipe is easily adapted to stainless steel or ceramic crocks. You will want the substrate weighted down throughout fermentation to press out any air pockets that form.

1⅔ cups dried soybeans

4 tablespoons sea salt, plus more for covering miso surface

1 tablespoon plus 2 teaspoons seed miso

4 cups plus 6 tablespoons koji

1. In a pot or bowl, add the dried soybeans and add enough water to cover the beans by 2 to 3 inches. Cover the pot or bowl with a lid or a cloth and set aside. Soak at room temperature overnight, for approximately 10 hours.

2. Using a colander, strain the water from the beans. Add the beans to a large pot and fill the pot with fresh water so that the beans are 2 to 3 inches below the water's surface. Bring to a boil over high heat. Reduce the heat to low and simmer for 4 hours, checking periodically to make sure the water level has not fallen below the surface of the beans. Do not worry about over-cooking the beans, but be sure that they are cooked well enough to mash. The beans should be easily crushed when you squeeze them between your fingers.

3. Strain the cooking water from the beans using a colander set over a bowl. Reserve 3 cups of the cooking liquid and set aside.

4. In a large bowl, mash the hot beans with a potato masher until completely smooth. A little bit at a time, add ¾ cup of the bean cooking liquid to the beans and stir until it forms a wet, creamy paste.

5. Add the salt and mix thoroughly.

jar with plastic bag

6. Cover with a clean cloth or lid and allow the mixture to cool to room temperature.

7. While your bean mixture is cooling, rinse your fermentation vessel or vessels with boiling water. Set aside, upside down on a clean surface.

8. When the bean mixture is sufficiently cool, mix the seed miso with 1 cup of the bean cooking liquid in a small bowl until evenly distributed. Add the seed miso mixture and the koji to the mashed beans and mix thoroughly. The mixture should feel slightly softer and looser than Play-Doh, but not runny. Add more of the reserved cooking liquid to reach this consistency, if necessary.

9. Form the mixture into balls a little smaller than tennis balls and throw them into the bottom of the fermentation vessel with a little force—you want them to splat against the bottom and sides of the

fermentation vessel, expelling as much air as possible and packing tightly. Once the thrown miso balls form one complete layer, make a fist and press it down with your knuckles, leaving no air pockets. Repeat this throwing and pressing process until the vessels have about an inch of headspace.

10. Sprinkle the surface of your miso with a good $\frac{1}{16}$-inch layer of sea salt.

11. Press a single layer of plastic wrap onto the entire salted surface of your miso and let the plastic wrap come up the sides a bit, pressed tightly to the walls. Cover the miso thoroughly, as you are creating an anaerobic environment in there! When we use jars with screw-on lids (like mason jars), we like to situate a large stone or a sealable plastic bag with enough water to take up the headspace between the miso and the lid. The stone or bag acts as a weight, constantly pushing down on the miso and squishing out bubbles that form. It also takes up real estate in the headspace, keeping oxygen interaction to a minimum. Repeat this process with any remaining jars.

12. Allow the miso to sit at room temperature for 4 weeks. You should see tiny bubbles form along the walls of your jars and because the lid is only loosely screwed on, there is no cause for concern that gases will build up and explode the jar. Alternatively, you could outfit your miso vessel with an air lock or use a Harsch-style crock.

At 4 weeks, uncover and taste your miso! It will be salty and sweet with a richness that can be likened to very mild cheese.

Here are some suggested variations.

In step 5, add a loosely packed cup of chopped dandelion greens and leeks.

For a quick and easy miso ferment, start the process at step 3 with cooked canned beans, like chickpeas. You may need to add additional water if starting with canned beans.

The liquid that forms on the surface of your miso as it ferments is tamari. Although it is difficult to get any quantity worth trying to save from a low-volume ferment, savor the couple of drops you can spoon off on a small ball of rice.

TEMPEH

Let go of what you think you know about tempeh and reimagine it. Start with a dense yet delicate mushroomy texture. Layer in a flavor that evokes rich nuts and clean, mild cheeses. Color the tempeh cloud-white and make it exquisitely soft. Now finish it off any number of ways: from deep-fried to oven-roasted. You can even eat it raw if it is fresh. Once fresh homemade tempeh sweeps you away, you will want to dress it up and down with all your favorite culinary tricks.

Tempeh was invented in Indonesia several hundred years ago when trade with China brought soybeans into contact with a fungus used in several traditional Indonesian ferments: *Rhizopus oligosporus*. Today, tempeh is made with a variety of legumes and grains. We've even fermented soba noodles with *Rhizopus* spores, then marinated the noodle tempeh and thrown it on skewers for a grill party! Our guests were totally impressed.

Once you get the hang of it, you can easily include tempeh-making as a weekly ritual with very little investment. The keys to successful tempeh fermentation are substrate choice and preparation, vessel choice, and temperature.

Most legumes and grains can be fermented with *Rhizopus oligosporus,* as long as the individual pieces aren't packed too densely; you need to ensure that air can flow in between them and that the hyphae, or the threads that make up the fungus, can penetrate them.

When choosing your substrate or substrates, you need to think in terms of size. Examples of legumes that are a good size to allow airflow are soybeans, black beans, pigeon peas, cannellini beans, yellow split peas, and large brown lentils. Examples of legumes that would be difficult to ferment into tempeh because they are quite small and would pack too densely are red lentils and petite beluga lentils. Because of their larger size, larger legumes are typically the backbone of tempeh ferments, and a lesser amount of small grain is mixed in to augment the flavor, texture, or nutritional value.

* * * * * * * *

For awesome substrate combinations, try chickpeas with pearl barley, black beans with brown rice, or cannellini beans with bulgur. To make a really outrageous tempeh, throw in some sesame seeds, flax seeds, sea veggies like arame or wakame, or add cumin or oregano. These won't inhibit the mycelium growth, as long as the moisture level of the overall substrate remains the same and space for airflow is protected.

* * * * * * * *

Use dried or fresh beans and grains for tempeh-making. Precooked products are most often overcooked and will turn to mush. Cook the beans and grains as you normally would in a pot with water. Some beans will require soaking prior to cooking. Add a splash of vinegar during cooking to acidify the substrate slightly and discourage unwanted bacterial growth. Take the beans off the heat a few minutes earlier than you normally would. They should still have structure so they don't fall apart during fermentation, but not be so hard that the hyphae can't get in there. This is best determined by taking a bite. You want to say to yourself, "I *could* eat them like this, but I'd prefer them a little softer"—that's when they are done. As the fermentation process will further break down their structure, you will arrive at just the right final consistency if the cooked substrate is slightly al dente.

Once the substrate is cooked, remove any tough hulls. The hulls of most grains break down during the cooking process, but legumes often have tougher hulls. Some legumes, like yellow split peas for instance, generally can be found hull-free, making this an easy choice for the home tempeh maker. You can quickly remove the hulls of other beans after cooking by squeezing the beans through your fingers or rubbing them between your hands. The hulls of most varieties will separate and pop right off. Each type of legume reacts a little differently, but you'll figure it out pretty quickly. Once the beans and hulls are separated, they will be all jumbled together. The easiest way to remove the free hulls from the mixture is to drop them back into the slightly acidified water, where the hulls will rise while the beans sink. You can then skim the hulls off the top with a slotted spoon. Be sure to stir the beans a few times to allow trapped hulls to rise to the surface.

For home tempeh-making, we often strain off the water using a colander and then spread the still-warm substrate out on a clean kitchen towel for a few minutes for the water to evaporate. Once the glossy wet look is gone, we proceed. You can also try a blow-dryer if you are making a larger batch. Either way, you are going for the same end result—moisture within the substrate, not *on* it. Your moist, cooked substrate is ready for fermenting when it is room temperature, there is no water on the outside, no water pooling at the bottom of the pot, and no slick, wet look.

When considering a vessel or form for making tempeh, pay special attention to the airflow around and throughout the substrate. The easiest way to ensure airflow both *to* and *through* the substrate is to use sandwich-size resealable plastic bags and perforate them every inch or so in a grid pattern, using a kitchen ice pick, a thick embroidery-style needle, or a knife with a pointed end. The holes in the bag regulate air movement while the bag limits the thickness of the substrate to about one inch. If you pack the substrate much thicker than this, air will have a hard time getting to the center of the substrate and it won't ferment properly. We have also fermented tempeh in muffin pans, pie pans, cookie cutters, and lots of other vessels by making the depth of the substrate about three-quarters of an inch and covering it with perforated aluminum foil. After a couple of rounds of tempeh fermentation, you'll get the hang of it and have the confidence to branch out. Just think airflow *to* and *through*.

The best temperature for your tempeh ferment is 88°F, but fluctuations between 82°F and 95°F are acceptable. Our favorite way to regulate the temperature is to get a cheap reptile thermostat and under-tank heat mat and stick it all in the oven (see Chapter 2: The Fermenter's Pantry). This setup shouldn't cost more than thirty dollars, and in fermentation, this is money well spent—the setup can be used for making a number of other ferments, like yogurt or room temperature ferments in the cold winter months. If you have a dehydrator on hand, this will work as well. But depending on how fast the fan goes, you may need to restrict the airflow to the substrate by, for example, poking holes in your bag every two inches instead of every one inch. You'll know you have too much airflow when the beans dry out around the holes instead of fermenting. Never set your tempeh directly on the heat source. It will overheat.

Tiny black spots may appear close to the air holes at around 24 hours of fermentation. This is sporulation and is not harmful in any way. In fact, it is these spores that are tempeh starter! Tempeh spores, or starter, can be obtained from a variety of sources. If you have a local tempeh-maker, they are a good place to start and are usually happy to share their spores with home fermenters. Starter can also be obtained online from a number of websites, including GEM Cultures. Once you have tempeh spores, they can be propagated, but it requires a high level of sterility in order to keep your culture strong and uncontaminated. For more information on propagating tempeh spores, refer to the fantastic book *The Book of Tempeh* by William Shurtleff and Akiko Aoyagi.

A very faint smell of ammonia may be barely detectable in perfectly healthy and safe tempeh. If the ammonia scent is obvious and strong, likely your tempeh overheated during fermentation, was too wet, or the substrate was too hot when the spores were added. Tempeh with a strong smell of ammonia should be discarded.

* * * * * * * *

YELLOW SPLIT PEA TEMPEH

Not only is this a really simple tempeh to make because the hulls of the split peas are already removed, but it has a delightful and earthy flavor. This is the tempeh we make most at home. People just starting out with tempeh making can have great success using yellow split peas in their initial tempeh efforts.

Yield: approximately 1 pound

1 cup dried yellow split peas

¼ teaspoon vinegar

⅛ teaspoon tempeh starter, or as per provider's instructions

1. In a large bowl, add split peas and 3 cups of fresh water. Soak split peas covered at room temperature for 8 to 12 hours (or overnight).

2. Drain off the soaking water. Put the split peas in a saucepan and add enough fresh water to cover them by 1½ inches.

3. Add the vinegar and bring the water to a boil over medium-high heat. Turn down the heat to low and simmer for 10 to 15 minutes or until peas are cooked al dente. If dense foam forms on the top, skim it off with a spoon. You want them to be just cooked through. If they are overcooked, they will mush together and good airflow will not be possible.

4. Drain off the cooking water in a colander. Flip the peas up and down in the colander to allow the moisture to escape through evaporation. Alternatively, pat them dry with a clean towel or use a blow-dryer to dry the peas while they are in the pot. The peas are dry enough either when there is no moisture visible on the bottom of the pot or when the surface of the peas no longer shines.

5. When the peas have cooled to body temperature, put them back in the pot and mix in the tempeh starter very well. When you think you have mixed enough, mix for another 30 seconds. About 2 minutes should do it.

6. Spread the peas about 1 inch thick in your tempeh form (page 103) and make sure there is some enough airflow, but not too much. A sealable plastic bag with needle holes poked every inch or so in a grid pattern provides just the right amount of air.

7. Incubate at 88°F for 24 hours. Between 12 and 16 hours, the process of fermentation will begin kicking off a lot of heat. At this point, your focus may switch from keeping it warm enough to keeping it cool enough. It is often necessary to turn off or remove the heat source if there is no thermostat controlling it.

8. You should have good tempeh in about 24 hours. The beans will be firmly bound in a white network of mycelium and will have a pleasant, crisp aroma. The entire cake of tempeh will be in one piece and you should be able to lift the whole thing without it bending or breaking. The best way to remove the tempeh from the bag is to cut it open with a knife. Place the tempeh in the refrigerator, but do not stack them if you made multiple cakes! Once cooled, the tempeh can be put into an airtight container or wrapped in foil. They will keep 4 to 5 days in the refrigerator or up to 3 months in the freezer.

* * * * * * * *

THE TEMPEHST'S ORANGE–GINGER TEMPEH OVER COCONUT RICE

Yield: 4 servings

MARINADE AND TEMPEH

1 cup orange juice

1 tablespoon lemon juice

2 tablespoons finely grated ginger

2 teaspoons minced garlic

½ cup tamari

1 tablespoon umeboshi vinegar

¾ tablespoon brown rice syrup

1 pound tempeh (fresh is best!), cut into ¾-inch chunks

COCONUT RICE

2 cups long-grain or brown jasmine rice

1 (13–14 ounce) can unsweetened coconut milk

1 (3-inch) cinnamon stick

1 bay leaf

¼ teaspoon salt

ADDITIONAL INGREDIENTS

2 tablespoons coconut oil

2 sprigs fresh basil or cilantro, for garnish (optional)

1. In a medium-size bowl, combine all the marinade ingredients except the tempeh and mix thoroughly. Add the tempeh chunks and stir or gently shake to ensure every piece is coated with marinade. Cover and set aside for 2 to 4 hours at room temperature, or overnight in the refrigerator. If you are in a hurry, simply simmer the marinade and tempeh in a saucepan over low heat for 25 minutes and proceed.

2. While the tempeh is marinating, rinse the rice in a sieve under cold running water 2 to 3 minutes, then drain well.

3. Warm a saucepan over medium heat and add the rice. Slowly stir the rice until it is dry and releases a toasty aroma. Stir in the coconut milk, 1 cup water, cinnamon, bay leaf, and salt and turn the heat up to high to bring to a boil. Reduce the heat to low and simmer, covered, for 20 minutes or until all liquid has been absorbed. Remove from the heat and let stand, covered, for 5 minutes. Discard cinnamon stick and bay leaf, and fluff rice with a fork.

4. Warm a skillet or wok over medium-high heat and add the coconut oil. Once the coconut oil heats up (about 1 minute or so), use a slotted spoon to remove the tempeh chunks from the marinade and place them in the heated oil. Cook only a few pieces at a time— if you add too many at once, it will decrease the temperature of the oil and your tempeh will become mushy. Cook without stirring until the bottom sides are browned, then flip and repeat on all sides. Remove and place tempeh on a paper bag or paper towel. Repeat until all pieces are browned and ready to eat.

5. Serve the tempeh on top of the coconut rice. Garnish with the fresh herbs, if desired, and devour! For a side dish, consider lightly oiled and grilled bok choy.

FERMENTED PORRIDGES

Porridges have migrated across meals to arrive on the breakfast table, but traditionally porridge was served as a side dish alongside meat and savory foods. Either way, fermenting your grains before consuming them will result in a more robust flavor, smoother texture, and nourishing meal that is easy to digest. *Ogi* is so easy to make— and requires such little preparation—that there is little reason not to. *Amazake* takes a bit more attention and preparation, but the sweet smell permeating your home on the morning you wake up to the finished product will make it all worthwhile.

Pretty much any whole grain can be fermented using the methods below. Once you learn the traditional recipes for amazake and ogi, try substituting oats or pearl barley. You won't be disappointed.

＊　＊　＊　＊　＊　＊　＊　＊

AMAZAKE

In this recipe, we use a rice cooker or a slow cooker, but if you have a more specific temperature-controlled device, such as a dehydrator or a heat mat with thermostat, you will get more consistent results without as much attention. See Chapter 2: The Fermenter's Pantry for more information about temperature control.

Yield: About 4 cups

½ cup brown rice

2½ cups koji (for more about koji, see Sweet White Miso page 96)

3-5 cups water

1. In a medium saucepan set over high heat, combine the rice with 3 cups of water. Bring to a boil, reduce the heat to low, and cover. Simmer for 45 minutes, or until rice is soft and porridge-like.

2. Using an instant-read thermometer, cool the mixture to below 140°F, then mix in the koji. If the mixture is on the dry side, add up to 2 cups water to make it more porridge-like. Place in either a rice cooker or slow cooker on the "warm" setting. Leave the lid partially open so heat can escape, and monitor the temperature to make sure it stays right around 140°F.

3. Ferment for 7 to 10 hours, stirring occasionally. The mixture should start to smell much sweeter after 2 hours, and will become progressively sweeter as it ferments. Depending on how you like it to taste, you can ferment it for up to 14 hours.

4. When the amazake is as sweet as you like it, turn off the rice cooker or slow cooker. Bring 2 cups of water to a boil in a medium saucepan set over high heat, and add the amazake to it. Bring the mixture back to a very gentle boil, then remove from the heat. It will be the consistency of oatmeal.

5. Serve warm with sliced banana and toasted black sesame seeds, or your favorite fruit-and-nut combination, for a delicious breakfast. Or put in an airtight container and keep in the refrigerator for up to 1 week.

* * * * * * * *

Amazake can be used as a healthy substitute for sweeteners in other recipes. Use it as a less-sweet replacement for honey or maple syrup. If substituting amazake for a dry sweetener like sugar or maple crystals, you will need to reduce the amount of milk or other liquid that the recipe calls for. Try it in pancakes!

* * * * * * * *

AMAZAKE SODA

Yield: Four 1½–cup servings

1 cup amazake (page 104)

4 tablespoons lime juice

4 cups soda water

Lime slices

Ice

1. In a blender, combine amazake and lime juice. Blend on high until smooth.

2. In a pitcher, combine amazake mixture with soda water. Stir gently to combine.

3. Add lime slices and ice and serve immediately.

✳ ✳ ✳ ✳ ✳ ✳ ✳ ✳

OGI MILLET PORRIDGE

This is a ferment we like to set up at the beginning of the week and eat daily until it is gone. Every day, the ogi will become more and more sour, and the consistency changes too! It never bores. Feel free to substitute other grains in this recipe as well. Some grains can be purchased already cracked, pearled, or rolled. For these, you can skip the first step.

WEEKLY

2 cups dried millet

4 cups water

DAILY

½ cup milk, plus more as needed

1 tablespoon maple syrup

Pinch of cinnamon

Chopped thyme, chopped nuts, hemp seeds, dried fruit, fresh fruit, yogurt (optional)

1. Coarsely grind millet in the dry canister of your blender. You could also use a repurposed coffee grinder and grind the millet in small batches, or grind it by hand using a mortar and pestle if you are looking for a little arm workout.

2. Combine the ground millet and water in a large swing-top jar. Close the lid and let it sit for 24 hours.

3. Pour off the water, being cautious not to pour off the grains along with it. You are not attempting to strain all the water off, just pouring off most of it. Using a spoon, remove about ½ cup of millet, tilting the spoon to the side to let more water drain off, and place the millet in a small saucepan with the milk, maple syrup, and cinnamon. Simmer over medium heat until porridge consistency is reached. For a creamier porridge, add more milk.

4. Remove from the heat and transfer to a bowl. Top with chopped thyme, nuts, seeds, fruit, yogurt, or any toppings that you wish.

5. Add 4 cups fresh water to the remaining millet in the swing-top jar. Close and set on counter for another 24 hours.

6. Repeat every day until it is gone! The ferment will continue to become more sour. Enjoy within a week.

FERMENTED DOUGHS

Sourdough was sparked alongside agriculture in the Fertile Crescent thousands of years ago. The two have always been inseparable. In every bag of whole or ground grains you buy, a superabundance of wild yeasts and lactic acid–forming bacteria lie in wait for a little bit of moisture to start their own growth. If you wonder at the powerful allure of a freshly baked sourdough loaf with a crackling crust and the perfect relationship between flavor and texture, contemplate your own spark, your own growth, your ancestral history, and your internal microbiota. It will all make sense.

If you are one of the lucky ones who cultivates a sourdough starter in your home fermenting kitchen, you will be able to imbue your baked, fried, and boiled breads with not only that craveable and complex sourdough flavor, but also all the health benefits that are bestowed upon grains that have undergone the fermentation process. From pizza crust to pancakes, from muffins to dumplings and bread kvass, break away from the habit of overusing chemical leaveners and purchased yeasts, and let wild yeast add some spark to your life!

To start and maintain a sourdough culture, all you need are flour and water. The yeast and lactic acid–forming bacteria responsible for the transformation are already present in the flour and in the environment. Depending on the varieties of wild yeast in the fields that the grain was grown in, in the mill that it was ground in, and your kitchen environment, you may wish to toss in a few raisins or grapes. This will add some additional varieties of yeast to the mix, and you'll have a robust, bubbly, pungent culture brewing. The lactic acid–forming bacteria don't seem to struggle in these cultures, so we have never heard of anyone having to add additional lacto-bacteria to their sourdough starter. Some people also like to feed their culture additional simple sugars like honey or apple juice, especially to revitalize an underfed culture or to speed up the fermentation process in preparation for using sourdough in a recipe.

There is lots of controversy and, often, lively debate about the proper ratio of water to flour to use when starting and maintaining a sourdough starter, as well as the correct flour to use and even the proper definition of sourdough. We have found that sourdough starters are all unique and have been selectively cultivated for different properties. You can use a variety of grain-based flours for your sourdough starter and in your sourdough recipes as well. We have even successfully made grain-free sourdough muffins with legume-based flours.

We keep a culture in our refrigerator and feed it weekly (approximately). You must plan in advance before using the culture, as most recipes require at least an overnight incubation period of a larger batch of sourdough. We have gone through phases where we use our sourdough culture more regularly. During one fun month, we made some form or fashion of sourdough pancakes every morning for breakfast, for instance. If you use your culture quite often, keep it on the counter and feed it of flour and water daily.

If your culture goes hungry for too long on the counter or in the refrigerator, it will form hooch on the surface. Hooch is a dark liquid that is somewhat alcoholic and smells that way. If hooch forms on the surface, pour it off and resume your normal feeding schedule—the culture should return to normal quickly. The health of the culture shouldn't be affected if this happens occasionally, but you will notice that the flavor and aroma of an underfed culture is not as awesome as one that is properly fed. It will smell and taste of acetic acid or alcohol. In the rare case that mold forms on your culture, discard the entire thing and start a new one; there is no need to mess around with a culture that has already expressed a weakness. As long as your sourdough starter remains mold free, it will last forever.

In addition to sourdough, there are a variety of other fermented doughs. In yet another example of fermentation's global and historical nature, different populations around the world have long cultured flour from local grains and legumes, resulting in an array of fermented doughs. In Ethiopia, injera sour flatbreads are made from teff flour and used either as the surface on which food is served (and subsequently ripped up and used as a spoon) or as a wrap to stuff with food like berbere-spiced lentils. Idli and dosa, soft-cooked doughs made from lentil and rice flours, are of Indian origin.

Idli is steamed, making plump dumplings, where dosa is more crepe-like and fried. Both are gluten-free and absolutely scrumptious. Idli are often eaten as a breakfast food along with chutney. Dosa are often served stuffed with masala, a spiced potato dish.

Once you get the hang of sourdough-style fermentation and some tried-and-true traditional recipes, you'll be ready for all sorts of global culinary adventures right in your kitchen. Below are the template sourdough starter we use at home and some ways we use it. Once you have a sourdough starter, the possibilities are endless, as are the resources for recipes. Following that are our must-try-at-home recommendations for other fermented flour culinary traditions.

* * * * * * * *

BASIC SOURDOUGH STARTER

This is a fast and loose kind of recipe. You are trying for a soft, doughy consistency that bubbles well and looks really alive.

Yield: About 4 cups, initially

4–6 cups all-purpose flour

6 raisins

1. Clean and dry a large jar or medium mixing bowl.

2. Make the initial sourdough starter by combining 1 cup of the all-purpose flour with ⅔ cup water in the vessel. Mix the batter until it's smooth, sticky, and thick, then stir in the raisins. Scrape any excess dough down the sides of the container, and loosely cover the vessel with plastic wrap or partially cover with a lid. Let the mixture rest at room temperature for 24 hours.

3. After 24 hours have passed, remove the raisins with a clean spoon and discard them. Now it's time to feed the starter. You will do this every 24 hours for the next 3 or 4 days. To feed the starter, add 1 cup of the all-purpose flour and ⅔ cup of water to your vessel. Mix until the batter is smooth, thick, and sticky; scrape down the sides; and cover loosely. By the third day, you should see bubbles beginning to form, and your starter should be increasing in size.

4. On the fifth or sixth day, your starter should be ready to use. It will smell pungent and sour, and there should be lots of bubbles by this point. Now you can use some of the starter for breads, pancakes, muffins, and more.

5. In order to maintain the starter, continue feeding it daily. If you aren't going to use the starter soon, cover it tightly and place it in your refrigerator. Take it out and feed it once a week (allowing it to sit at room temperature for 24 hours before placing it back in the refrigerator).

If you have more starter than you need, you can give some away, make pancakes and either eat them or freeze them for later, or use some of it to start other ferments. Sourdough starter makes excellent starter for bread kvass (page 127).

✳   ✳   ✳   ✳   ✳   ✳   ✳   ✳

MILD SOURDOUGH RYE

Sourdough rye breads come in many styles, from moist and dense to dry and cracker-like. This recipe makes dense, moist bread that has great flavor and is perfect sliced thinly and topped with cold cuts and mustard, butter and jam, or cucumber and cream cheese with a bit of dill. You'll want to feed your sourdough starter the day before starting this recipe with at least 2 cups of flour (and the requisite water), so you can have a robust and active starter for this recipe while also leaving some starter behind for future creations.

Yield: 2 loaves

2 cups sourdough starter

3 ¼ cups water

4 cups rye flour

1 tablespoon salt

1 ½ cups all-purpose flour

1. In a large bowl, combine sourdough starter, 4 cups rye flour, and 2¼ cups of water. Mix well. Cover with aluminum foil or plastic wrap and allow to sit at room temperature for roughly 12 hours.

2. Add the salt, all-purpose flour, and 1 cup of water. Mix gently until thoroughly combined.

3. Pour the batter-like dough, dividing it equally, into two 8 × 4-inch nonstick loaf pans. Cover the pans with aluminum foil or plastic wrap and let stand at room temperature for 3 hours.

4. Preheat oven to 325°F. Bake, uncovered, for 1½ hours; an internal thermometer will read 190°F or a little higher when it is done.

5. Remove the loaves from the oven and wrap in clean kitchen towels to cool for a few hours, then slice and serve. This bread will stay fresh for 4 to 5 days wrapped in paper on the counter, or it can be frozen for up to 3 months.

❋ ❋ ❋ ❋ ❋ ❋ ❋ ❋

SIMPLE SOURDOUGH PANCAKES

Be sure to feed the starter the night before, so that it is quite thick. Also, make sure you have enough starter for this recipe, as well as some left afterward to perpetuate the culture.

Yield: 6–8 pancakes

2 eggs

1½ cups sourdough starter

½ teaspoon baking soda

1 teaspoon maple syrup

Pinch of salt

Pinch of cinnamon (optional)

Butter, viili, fresh fruit (optional)

1. Preheat a cast-iron or nonstick skillet over medium heat.

2. In a medium bowl, beat the eggs until combined. Whisk in the starter, baking soda, maple syrup, salt, and cinnamon, if using, until the batter is smooth.

3. Once the skillet is very hot, ladle about ¼ cup of batter per pancake into the skillet. Cook until bubbles start to form on the surface and the edges are visibly cooked. Using a spatula, carefully flip the pancakes and cook the other side until golden brown.

4. Serve with butter, viili, fresh fruit, and/ or maple syrup.

If sweet is not your thing, omit the maple syrup and cinnamon and make the pancakes savory by throwing a handful of fresh herbs, chopped bacon, and / or scallions into the batter.

✳ ✳ ✳ ✳ ✳ ✳ ✳ ✳

INJERA

Making the culture is part of this recipe. If used regularly, the culture can be maintained like a sourdough starter. Serve injera flatbread with Berbere-Spiced Lentils (page 112).

Yield: About 4 large pancakes

1½ cups teff flour

2 cups water

¼ teaspoon salt

½ teaspoon baking powder

Coconut oil or organic canola oil, for frying

1. Put the teff flour in a large bowl. Add the water and stir well, until the batter is smooth. Loosely cover the bowl with a cloth and allow to ferment at room temperature, undisturbed, for 24 to 72 hours.

2. Bubbles should begin to form in the batter after 24 hours—if there aren't any bubbles, let the mixture ferment longer. It may grow larger in volume and start to look kind of like a brain on the surface. This is a normal sign that the fermentation is active.

3. When the batter is sour and bubbly, stir in the salt and baking powder; mix very well, so that the baking powder disperses evenly throughout the batter. The batter will lose some of its volume when you stir it—that's ok.

4. Heat a large cast-iron or nonstick skillet over medium heat, and coat with coconut oil or canola oil. Pour enough batter into the pan to just coat the flat surface, then cover and cook for about 4 minutes, or until the top of the injera is dry and has small bubbles in it. The cover is important, as it keeps moisture in (otherwise the injera may crack).

5. Place the injera on a piece of parchment paper, then repeat with the remaining batter, layering the finished injera between more pieces of parchment paper.

6. To serve, lay warm injera flat on a plate or other large serving surface, like a wooden cutting board. Spoon a serving of berbere-spiced lentils or another Ethiopian dish in a mound on top of the injera. To eat, rip off small sections of the injera and use it to scoop up the lentils by hand.

Alternatively, you can use the injera flatbread to roll up a variety of other ingredients. We've been known to make tuna salad wraps with injera flatbreads.

* * * * * * * *   * * * * * * * *

BERBERE—SPICED LENTILS

Yield: 4 servings

1 cup red lentils

4 tablespoons butter

1 small yellow onion, finely chopped

4 cloves garlic, minced

2 tablespoons Berbere Spice Blend

1 small tomato, cored and chopped

Kosher salt

Injera flatbread (page 111)

1. Rinse the lentils in a strainer under cold running water and allow to drain.

2. In a medium, heavy-bottom saucepan, heat the butter over medium heat. Add the onion, stirring occasionally until golden brown, about 3 minutes. Add the garlic and cook for about 1 minute or until fragrant, stirring constantly to prevent burning.

3. Add the lentils, berbere spice blend, tomato, and 4 cups of water to the saucepan. Turn the heat up to high and bring to a boil, then reduce the heat to medium-low. Simmer uncovered, stirring occasionally, until the stew is thick and the lentils are tender, about 30 minutes. Season with salt to taste, and serve on or in injera flatbread.

BERBERE SPICE BLEND

Yield: ½ cup

2 teaspoons whole coriander seeds

1 teaspoon whole fenugreek seeds

½ teaspoon black peppercorns

¼ teaspoon whole allspice berries

Seeds from 6 cardamom pods

4 whole cloves

½ cup dried onion flakes

⅛ teaspoon cayenne pepper (or more to taste)

3 tablespoons paprika

2 teaspoons kosher salt

½ teaspoon ground nutmeg

½ teaspoon ground ginger

½ teaspoon ground cinnamon

1. In a small, dry pan, toast the coriander, fenugreek, peppercorns, allspice, cardamom, and cloves over medium heat, stirring occasionally. When the spices are fragrant, remove from heat and allow to cool.

2. In a spice grinder or mortar and pestle, combine the toasted whole spices with the onion flakes, cayenne pepper, paprika, salt, nutmeg, ginger, and cinnamon. Grind all ingredients to a fine powder. Store in an airtight jar in the refrigerator for up to a month.

Idli and dosa

The soft, velvety feel of idli and dosa is coaxed from the rice and split black lentils, or urad dal, through soaking and grinding, then fermenting the grain and legume. Traditionally served for breakfast in India and topped with chutney, the savory cakes are the pride of the Indian home, and making them soft and cloud-like is an art form. The following recipes are compiled from numerous cookbooks and websites. We have found idli and dosa recipes that claim great success using whole black lentils, yogurt, semolina, rice that is not parboiled, and/or *poha* (a flattened rice). We selected the ingredients and processes listed below for ease of sourcing and preparing—and for their sumptuous result.

❋ ❋ ❋ ❋ ❋ ❋ ❋ ❋

IDLI

To make idli, you will need an idli form. Traditionally, idli trays, or trees, are filled with the batter and steamed to make the proper soft, round shape. We have found that on a budget, you can get away with using a mini muffin pan, as long as you have a pot large enough to place it in for steaming. And if not, you can preheat the oven to 350°F, place the muffin tin on the rack of a roasting pan, fill the bottom of the pan with boiling water, and cover the pan with either a lid or an aluminum foil tent. Bake in the oven for about 20 minutes, or until a toothpick stuck in the middle of an idli comes out clean. The shape may not be spot-on, but if you aren't making idli regularly—or trying to impress someone who appreciates a true-to-form, traditional idli—it works in your favor, in regard to both your kitchen storage and your wallet.

Yield: Approximately 36 idli (serves 4–6)

½ cup split black lentils (urad dal)

½ teaspoon fenugreek seeds

1½ cups parboiled rice (ukda chawal)

⅛ teaspoon salt

Coconut oil, for greasing

Chopped cilantro, Rhubarb Chutney (page 80), yogurt, or viili (optional)

1. In the morning, combine the split black lentils and fenugreek seeds in a bowl. Fill with water to cover the mixture with at least an inch of water. Place the parboiled rice in a separate bowl and fill with enough water to cover the rice with at least an inch of water. Cover both bowls and set aside for 3 to 5 hours.

2. Drain off the water from the lentil mixture using a fine-mesh strainer. Put the mixture in a blender, add ⅓ cup of water, and blend, first on a low setting and gradually increasing to high, until the batter is smooth. You may need to add additional water to keep the mixture moving, keep the blender from overheating, and to obtain the proper consistency; add it little by little up to an additional ¼ cup. The consistency you are going for is light, fluffy, and pancake batter–like. Pinch a little bit of batter between two fingers and rub them together. The batter should not feel grainy, but smooth. When the desired consistency is reached, put the batter into a large bowl, scraping the sides with a spatula, then rinse out the blender.

3. Drain off the water from the rice using a fine mesh strainer and repeat the blending step as described in step 2, starting off with 2 cups of water and adding more as needed, up to an additional ½ cup. Once the batter is smooth, add it to the lentil batter and mix well. Cover and set aside in a warm location until the following morning.

4. The next morning, the mixture will smell a bit sour and will have doubled in size. Add the salt and mix gently so as not to cause the batter to fall.

5. Grease your idli form with the coconut oil. Fill each little cup with the batter, a little less than ¼ cup. Refrigerate any extra batter for making dosa.

6. Steam the batter-filled idli form in a closed pot with a few inches of water on the bottom for about 20 minutes, or until a toothpick stuck into the middle of an idli comes out clean.

7. Serve warm with chopped cilantro and Rhubarb Chutney (page 80), and perhaps a dollop of yogurt or viili, if you have some around. They are best eaten fresh, but idli can be stored in the fridge overnight and even frozen for later use. To reheat idli, steam them.

8. Cover any leftover idli batter and store it in the fridge to make dosas the next day.

* * * * * * *

In our kitchen, we don't always play by the rules. We have been known to toss fresh herbs, spices, and even chopped up dried fruit and nuts into idli and dosa batter before cooking. Idli batter also makes a wonderful shepherd's pie filling and/or topping. On incredibly lazy mornings, we have even cooked idli batter in a pot, stirring often like grits, and served fried eggs over it and a salad on the side. This fermented, gluten-free batter is easy to digest and goes well with all sorts of fare.

* * * * * * *

* * * * * * * *

DOSA

Yield: About 15 dosa (serves 4–6)

DOSA

½ onion, cut from pole to pole

Coconut oil, for frying

4 cups idli batter (pagse 113-114, steps 1-4)

2 cups home-fried potatoes and onions

OPTIONAL GARNISHES

Fermented Rhubarb Chutney (page 80)

Chopped cilantro

Yogurt

1. Heat a cast-iron or nonstick skillet over medium-high heat. Dip the onion in the coconut oil and use it to smear the oil on the surface of the pan.

2. In a medium-size bowl, gently stir together the idli batter and enough water to thin the batter to a crepe batter–like consistency, add approximately ¾ cup. You may wish to test a little bit of the batter in the skillet before cooking the entire batch. It should flatten out like a thin crepe.

3. Use a ladle to spoon about 2 tablespoons of batter onto the greased skillet. Immediately use the back of the ladle to spread the batter into an approximately 4-inch circle. Once the edges start to brown, flip the cake and cook for another 30 seconds. It might take you a few tries to get the thinness just right so the dosa doesn't fall apart when flipped.

4. Flip the dosa once again. Immediately spoon 2 tablespoons of potatoes and onions over half the dosa, then fold the other half over it. Let it cook for about 30 more seconds, then remove to plate. Garnish with chopped cilantro and/or yogurt.

5. Repeat until the batter is used up.

~ part three ~

DRINK

"WHAT CONTEMPTIBLE SCOUNDREL HAS STOLEN
THE CORK TO MY LUNCH?"
—W.C. FIELDS

Fermented beverages are sustenance, refreshment, and social lubrication for humans and many other species. In fact, scholars today believe that not only have humans evolved alongside fermented beverages, but also that alcohol, present to some degree in most fermented beverages, was the galvanizing substance that encouraged humans to become civilized. History has been shaped while beverages bubbled and brewed in crocks, jugs, and silos. From grain beers to fruit wines, sweet to sour, light to strong, not only do people desire these delicious and refreshing ferments, but some would argue that society needs them in order to produce the social intermingling and great inventiveness necessary for civilization to grow and thrive.

Throughout human civilization, fermented beverages have been made with almost any nutrient on this planet. Fruit, grain, herb, vegetable, nut, seed, root, and leaf all have their place in recipes for fermented beverages. These substrates either contain innate sugars or are mixed with a sugar source to encourage the growth of natural or cultured yeasts and/or bacteria. Like all fermentation, this process changes the nutrients in the substrate in many different ways. Liquids go from sweet to sour, clear to cloudy, flat to bubbly. The science of brewing up a fermented beverage is easy, but mastering the physical process takes practice and sometimes a few pieces of specialized equipment. Although it takes time to become a master, with a few simple items you can turn sugary liquids into delicious fermented brews without hassle.

Fermented beverages range in flavor, alcohol level, and amount of technical expertise required to make them. Variations in the curated environment that you set up for the microbes to do their work will determine where on the spectrum of these qualities your ferment will rest. Conditions such as the sugar available to the microbes at the various stages of fermentation, the number of microbes present at the start of each stage, the temperature of the fermentation, the duration of the process, and the oxygen levels in the solution are all conditions that will help guide the recipe and affect the taste, texture, alcohol content, and nutritive qualities of your finished brew.

STAGES OF BEVERAGE FERMENTATION

In general, beer and wine makers use specific language to describe the various stages of creating the alcohol content, flavor profile, and effervescence (or lack thereof) in different styles of beer and wine. The rules of each stage can be extrapolated and applied, singularly or in combination, to pretty much any fermented beverage to produce unique and delicious results. Take note that the terms "secondary fermentation" and "bottle conditioning" are often confused. The recipes in this section use the language explained below, so familiarize yourself with the terms. See Chapter 2: The Fermenter's Pantry for the specific equipment involved.

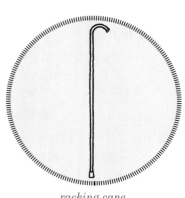

racking cane

Primary fermentation

In beer and wine, this is the most active phase of fermentation where the yeasts—and, if involved, the bacteria—do the majority of their transformative work. Primary fermentation in beer and wine is usually oxygen-rich in the beginning, but must be carefully protected from overoxygenation as it progresses. Some primary fermentation occurs in open-air vessels (covered with a cloth to protect it from unwanted invaders) or in vessels sealed with an air-lock system that allows gases to escape but not enter the vessel. When a beverage is finished with primary fermentation, it is fermented and ready to drink. But many recipes use additional steps to round out the flavor and adjust the effervescence.

Secondary fermentation

Some recipes that produce specific styles of beer or wine call for a secondary round of fermentation, most often in a low-oxygen environment with a low population of microbes. When the fermented liquid is gently transferred to secondary fermentation, most of the yeast and bacterial sediment—or lees—is left on the bottom of the primary fermentation vessel. This process is called "racking." When transferring liquid to your secondary vessel, you will want to do so with as little turmoil as possible to reduce the amount of oxygen that gets introduced. To do this at home, you can use a racking cane, which is easy and affordable. Secondary fermentation has a rounding and balancing effect on flavor and is used in our recipes for wines, ciders, and meads. Occasionally, we come across recipes that use subsequent steps (tertiary fermentation, etc).

In our home fermenting kitchen, we have not found any advantage to doing these on a small scale.

Bottle conditioning

Once your beverage has sufficiently fermented in primary and/or secondary fermentation, you can allow the beverage to condition within the bottle. This is the last stage before you drink the beverage. For different styles of beverages, this can mean different things. For example, a very dry wine that is no longer producing lees can be handled in a few ways. First, you could add more sugar and yeast before bottling; during bottle conditioning, fermentation would be instigated again in the closed vessel, leading to a boom of bubbles and a different flavor profile from the one you tasted before bottle conditioning. Second, you could simply bottle the wine as-is and age it, allowing the flavors that were already created to mellow and merge. This wine will further clarify, resulting in a mature wine whose qualities have been refined by the process. During the bottle-conditioning stage, home brewers might also choose to add things like sugar, pH adjusters, tannins, or pectic enzymes to encourage a ferment in the direction of their desired finish.

ALCOHOL BY VOLUME

Although many fermented beverages have been designed to contain higher amounts of alcohol, many have very little alcohol and are not only great for refreshment throughout the day, but also fun for children! Take a look at the table showing average amounts of alcohol by volume found in common beverages. Take note that even nonfermented beverages also have a small amount of spontaneously occurring alcohol. We included these as reference points.

"Nonalcoholic" is a legal term used to describe foods and beverages that fall below a certain alcohol by volume (ABV). In the United States, that ABV is usually set at 0.5%. Many fruit juices are exempted from this decree, as naturally occurring alcohol levels are often higher. Even force-carbonated, mass-marketed fountain sodas contain some amount of alcohol. Most open-air or loosely covered beverage ferments will fall into the nonalcoholic or very low–alcohol categories because the alcohol is allowed to evaporate off as it is produced, and these ferments often contain bacteria that transform the remaining alcohol into acids. During bottle conditioning, alcohol levels will likely rise, especially in ferments that have a high yeast count, like bread kvass, kefir, kombucha, and anything you pitch yeast into. If you are looking for a very low–alcohol beverage, try ferments that are principally lactic-acid forming, like lacto-lemonade or beet kvass.

AVERAGE AMOUNTS OF ALCOHOL BY VOLUME IN COMMON BEVERAGES

Lemon-lime soda, ginger ale, beet kvass, fruit punch	0.05–0.1%
Kombucha, water kefir, tepache	0.1–1.5%
Chhaang	2–3%
Hard cider	3–4%
Lager beer	4–5%
Dark beer	5–7%
Ginger beer	7–9%
White wine	10–11%
Mead	9–15%
Red wine	12–16%
Liqueur	20–24%
Hard liquor	38–40%

Most fermented beverages utilize some variety of yeast. The nature of all yeasts is to produce some amount of alcohol; the amount will vary depending on the strain of yeast, the substrate, and other conditions, like the presence of alcohol-transforming bacteria—for example, the aceto-forming bacterial strains found in kombucha. In addition to producing alcohol, yeasts are also CO_2 factories that give many fermented beverages their effervescence. A few recipes in this book, such as Lacto-Lemonade with whey (page 128) and Basic Beet Kvass (page 127) do not overemphasize yeast. If you want beverages with exceptionally low levels of alcohol, use these recipes as the backbone for your experiments.

Popular trends show that fermented drinks are consumed not only for basic sustenance or the alcohol content, but for functional benefits as well. Powerful probiotics, vitamins, minerals, healthy acids, and natural enzymes are well-known components of fermented beverages. In fact, many commercial beverage makers are taking steps to add to nonfermented beverages laboratory-derived ingredients that emulate what naturally occurs in fermented drinks. Next time you go to the grocery store, pay attention to the drink shelf and specifically to drink labels. You might be shocked to find that most of what you see there falls into the "functional beverage" category—Frankenstein beverages made from the addition of various powders and isolates that purport to enhance the nutritive quality of a beverage. This trend is not only strong but ever-growing too, as the drink shelf becomes larger and marketing money is funneled into this category.

It seems obvious to us that consumers are craving the complex and deeply nourishing effect of fermented beverages, and beverage businesses are scrambling to provide a surrogate. Fermented beverages are the original functional beverage with an unfathomably dense nutritional profile that fueled humankind's technological development and our highest achievements—from domestication of animals to fields of grain and from fine art to high finance. This cannot be duplicated in a sterile manufacturing plant using isolates and derivatives. Try fermenting beverages; you will be enlivened.

In our home fermenting kitchen, our main goals are ease and variety. From time to time, perhaps quarterly, we dabble in more sophisticated recipes for wine and beer. But we don't make a huge project out of every ferment—many delicious fermented beverages can be made in a regular kitchen and without a lot of fuss. The recipes we have included here have been selected with this in mind. Many other books and resources spell out, in great detail, highly specialized and sophisticated instructions for making different styles of beer and wine.

* * * * * * * *

BEER, WINE, CIDER, MEAD, SODA
What's the difference?

The truth is, these categories have a lot of overlap. For example, beer is defined in numerous ways. One definition is that it is a fermented beverage, alcoholic or nonalcoholic, made from cereal grains. Another definition is that the beer category covers a variety of beverages, both alcoholic and not, made from roots, molasses, or sugar; and yeast. Additionally, beverage ferments from a variety of cultural and geographical distinctions—such as pineapple-based Mexican *tepache*—have been linguistically lumped in with beer. For our purposes, we have generally followed the cultural definitions to assign categories.

* * * * * * * *

chapter 6

∽ KOMBUCHA, KEFIR, KVASS, AND OTHER ∽ LOW–ALCOHOL FERMENTED SODAS

Soda is the modern standard for refreshment. Served at almost every restaurant, bar, and event space in the world, it is the top-performing category in the beverage market. Why is soda so popular? We are convinced that it taps into the evolutionary heritage we discussed, in the Introduction. Soda's predecessors, fermented beverages and carbonated mineral water, were around long before the advent of soda. These two are similar to one another in that they are rich in nutrients and have a fine effervescence. These healthy, natural beverages were a part of daily life and as early as the seventeenth century, soda entrepreneurs caught on to these desirable qualities and tried to copy their characteristics. The resulting liquids were force-carbonated and flavored with various ingredients and sweeteners. As time marched on, this soda craze was such a hit that nonalcoholic force-carbonated beverages are now far more commonplace than their naturally occurring, health-giving predecessors. Many blame modern sodas in whole or in part for myriad diseases and disorders that now plague Western society. Skip the soda aisle, and ferment a natural, healthy, and deliciously bubbly refreshment with fresh ingredients from the farmer's market or your favorite produce vendor.

When making fermented soda—or anything carbonated, for that matter—you need to pay attention to the level of carbonation being produced at different stages and the type of bottle used. If the soda is allowed to ferment too long in a sealed vessel, it can rupture or explode. If the vesel is glass, this will be not only a sticky mess, but a dangerous mess. To protect yourself, get to know your ferment in plastic soda bottles first. They will get rock hard when ready, which will let you know it's time to put the bottles in the fridge. After the soda is fermented and chilled, don't let a sealed bottle come back to room temperature, as it is still at risk of overfermenting. By refrigerating the bottles after fermentation, you will stabilize the existing carbonation and slow the process down considerably. But regardless, slowly open your bottles over the sink to allow pressure and any runoff to drain away without making a mess. Once you get the knack for timing, you can make the transition to glass.

Our favorite recipes are probably your favorites too. There are an infinite number of variations to try here, so use these recipes as your guide, not your rule. Just keep in mind the balance of microbial type, sugar content, temperature, and time, and you will be drinking delicious, healthy fermented soda for years to come.

YEASTY BACTERIAL SODAS: REJUVELAC, KVASS, LACTO-LEMONADE

Sodas made from both lactic acid–forming bacteria and yeast make low-alcohol, acidic, and deliciously refreshing beverages. You don't need any special cultures to make these recipes at home. The sodas can be either inoculated by the natural yeasts and bacteria already present on your fresh raw ingredients (as in rejuvelac and beet kvass), or inoculated by a ferment you already have in your kitchen (as in bread kvass and lacto-lemonade). And remember, the sky's the limit! Take these recipes, apply them to what you love, and reap the rewards of an easy-to-make healthy soda.

Rejuvelac

Ann Wigmore was a healthy-living enthusiast and teacher who believed in the healing powers of sprouted grains. Born in 1909 in Lithuania, she contributed several healthful additions to the plates and cups of Westerners, including sprouts of all sorts. Rejuvelac was Wigmore's invention, adapted from a Romanian fermented grain drink, and is one of the cornerstones of her healthy-living prescription.

The process of making this sweet-and-sour drink begins with sprouting dry whole grains, which are then fermented. The sprouted grains can be used for two cycles of rejuvelac fermentation, but it is not recommended that you use them for a third round; their nutrients begin depleting and the flavor profile turns in an undesirable direction.

We love rejuvelac in our home fermenting kitchen. We not only drink it fresh with a squeeze of lemon or a bit of crushed fresh mint, but we use it in recipes like soups and braises. We also use it to inoculate new ferments.

❊ ❊ ❊ ❊ ❊ ❊ ❊ ❊

REJUVELAC

Yield: 1 quart

1 cup wheat berries, rye berries, spelt berries, or hulled barley

Vessel: 1-quart glass jar with lid and cloth cover

Duration: 6 to 7 days

1. Clean the vessel with soap and water. Place the grains in the jar and fill the jar with water. Cover with a cloth, secured with a rubber band, and allow it to sit at room temperature for 24 hours.

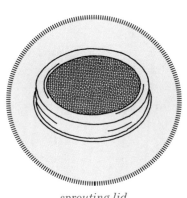

sprouting lid

2. Remove the cloth and cover the jar with a sprouting lid or cheesecloth and a rubber band. Drain the water from the jar. Stand the jar upside down, but at an angle (so that the remaining water can drip out and air can circulate in) in a bowl and allow to sit at room temperature for 12 hours.

3. Rinse the grains with fresh water, drain, and let stand for another 12 hours. Continue rinsing and draining the grains every 12 hours until you see little sprouts appear on the ends of the grains. This usually takes about 2 days.

4. Once the sprouts have appeared on the grains, rinse them one final time and then fill the jar with water. Allow to stand at room temperature, loosely covered with a lid, for 3 days. The water should get cloudy, and there will be lots of bubbles. Strain off the grains and reserve them. Cover the jar tightly and place in the fridge. After a few days, the beverage should have some natural carbonation.

5. You can reuse the grains for a second round of fermentation—just cover them with water and allow to sit at room temperature again. This time, the beverage should be ready after just 1 day of fermentation.

6. Serve the rejuvelac cold. It will keep in the refrigerator for up to a month.

Sprouting lids are mesh constructions made to screw onto standard jars. Sprouting lids can be made of stainless steel, plastic, and even ceramic. The mesh allows the contents of the jar to breathe and also allows water to drip out when the jar is propped upside down at an angle. Sprouting lids can be found in well-stocked kitchen supply stores, health food stores, and online.

Kvass

With its deep, rich red color and its sublime flavors that fuse earthiness with just the right amount of salt, sweet, and sour, beet kvass is something we make often in our home fermenting kitchen. Bread kvass is akin to the refreshment one might find in a light wheat beer on a summery afternoon. With Eastern European origins, both beet and bread kvass were likely popularized as safer alternatives to drinking plain water, which could be contaminated. As discussed earlier in the Introduction, fermentation virtually wipes out the possibility of contamination, even when the offending microbes are already present.

Kvass is purported to have liver-toning effects; it is also a folk remedy for kidney stones and indigestion. Drink these ferments flat or cap them for bottle conditioning, which makes a sparkling delight.

* * * * * * * *

BASIC BEET KVASS

Yield: ½ gallon

3 medium organic beets

2 teaspoons sea salt

½ gallon water

Vessel: ½-gallon glass jar with lid

Duration: 3 to 6 days

1. Clean the vessel and lid. Cut the unpeeled beets into 1½-inch dice. Place them in the jar.

2. Dissolve the sea salt in the water, and pour over the beets. Cover the jar with a loose-fitting lid and allow to ferment at room temperature for 3 to 5 days. If any scum forms on the surface, skim it off. You should see small bubbles forming in the liquid.

3. When the kvass is fermented to your liking, strain off the liquid and transfer to a sealable jug. You can either place in the refrigerator for drinking or allow to bottle condition for 24 hours at room temperature in a suitable vessel such as a swing-top glass bottle.

4. The beets can be used up to two more times to make kvass—when you've strained off the finished kvass, mix more salt and water and repeat the process. The kvass will ferment faster the second time around, especially if you pour in a little bit of fermented kvass to provide a higher initial microbe count.

After the beets have fermented a few rounds of kvass, use them in other recipes. Shred them to top off a salad, slice them and toss them in the juices of oranges and ginger for a refreshing side dish slaw, or use them to replace raw beets in borscht.

* * * * * * * *

BREAD KVASS

Yield: ½ gallon

5 slices rye or sourdough bread (stale is fine)

2 tablespoons honey

2 tablespoons sourdough starter or 2 cups plain kombucha

2 raisins

Vessel: ½-gallon glass jar with cloth cover

Duration: 6 days

1. Heat oven to 350°F. Cut the slices of bread into large chunks and place on a baking sheet. Toast the bread chunks in the oven for about 5 minutes or until they are completely dry and break like crackers.

2. Boil ½ gallon of water. Put the bread in a bowl, pour the boiling water over the bread, and steep for 1 hour. Strain off the liquid, squeezing the bread to get as much liquid out of it as possible. Discard the bread and allow the liquid to cool to room temperature.

3. Put the strained and cooled liquid into the vessel. Add the honey and the sourdough starter or kombucha. Cover with a cloth and allow to ferment at room temperature for 24 hours. If you notice any foam, scoop it off and discard it.

4. Strain the liquid through a fine-mesh sieve or cheesecloth. Pour the liquid into a sealable bottle and add raisins. Seal the bottle and place in the refrigerator for 4 days. After 4 days, the beverage should have some effervescence. Open, drink, and enjoy!

Kombucha, kefir, yogurt whey, sourdough starter, or juice from a lactic acid–forming vegetable ferment are all fair starters for ferments that require a separate inoculation step. When using kombucha or kefir for this inoculation, you may need to use a bit more than you would with other, more microbe-dense starters like whey and sauerkraut juice.

---

* * * * * * * *

LACTO-LEMONADE

Sadly, powders and food colorings have dominated the lemonade market for the past few decades. Show your neighborhood the power of real, fresh lemons and serve lacto-lemonade at your next lemonade stand! A fun alternative to a summer favorite, lacto-lemonade can be served as is or with fresh lavender, mint, or ginger to add a bit of sophistication to the mix.

Yield: About ½ gallon

¼ cup honey

3½ cups filtered water, warm

Juice of 5 medium lemons or limes

2 cups kombucha or 1 cup whey, sauerkraut juice, or beet kvass

Vessel: ½-gallon jar with cloth cover

Duration: 3 to 4 days

1. Dissolve honey in 3 cups of the filtered warm water in the ½-gallon jar. Add the citrus juice, plus another ½ cup filtered water. Allow the mixture to cool to room temperature, then add the kombucha, whey, sauerkraut juice, or kvass.

2. Cover the jar with a cloth, secure with a rubber band, and allow to ferment at room temperature for 3 days. You should see bubbles start to form on the surface of the liquid, and there may be thicker sediment at the bottom of the liquid. After 3 days, transfer to a sealable jug and either bottle condition for 1 day at room temperature or put directly in the fridge. Enjoy cold!

YEAST-PITCHED SODAS

Another way to get your soda going—and going fast—is to pitch yeast into the substrate, cap it, and let it go for about 24 hours. The result is a boisterous and very bubbly ferment without the acidic quality. Lots of bang, lots of flavor, lots of ease. These sodas are fun and totally worth making, but don't expect the health benefits of lacto-fermentation in these recipes. Do, however, expect an endless array of possibilities.

The process of making soda is just as simple as the drink itself. A nutrient-dense flavoring agent and sugar will make up the substrate. The equipment needed to make this type of soda is also simple. A couple of repurposed clean soda bottles will do just fine. Beyond that, you might need a pot to mix up the ingredients in and a spoon to mix them with. Yeast-pitched soda is definitely a low-investment home-brewer's dream.

Below is the basic soda recipe for 1 liter of unflavored soda followed by some suggested flavorings and their proportions. You can use these as templates for flavors of your own

design. Ingredients can be juiced, pureed, macerated, crushed, or tossed in whole for various effects. Use a 1-liter plastic soda bottle the first couple of times you make a recipe to get the hang of how fast it goes in your particular environment. Temperature is key here. At warmer temperatures, you will have a fully fermented beverage in less than 12 hours. At cooler temperatures, this could take up to 48 hours. Once you know how the yeast reacts to the specific substrate in your particular environment, you can switch to glass and set a timer so you don't wind up with exploding bottles!

Be sure to open the bottle slowly over the sink when you open it for the first time! Even after refrigeration, the natural effervescence can catch you off guard.

* * * * * * * *

BASIC YEAST–PITCHED SODA

Yield: 1 liter

4 tablespoons sugar

¼ teaspoon baker's or champagne yeast

Flavoring agents

Vessel: 1-liter plastic soda bottle

Duration: 12 to 48 hours

1. In a large pot, warm the sugar and 1 liter of water over medium heat, stirring constantly, until all the sugar has dissolved. At this point, you can also add any flavoring agents to gently cook them, or you can wait until step 3 to add raw ingredients.

2. Remove from heat, cover, and allow the sugar solution to cool to room temperature.

3. Once the solution has cooled, transfer it to the bottle, add the yeast and any other ingredients you wish to add, tightly cap the bottle, and gently shake to distribute the yeast.

4. Allow to ferment at room temperature until the bottle is firm and tight, giving only slightly when squeezed.

5. Transfer the bottle to the refrigerator and enjoy within 2 weeks. If you don't consume the entire bottle when you first open it, transfer the remaining amount into a smaller bottle that just accommodates the volume, cap tightly, and put back in the fridge. This will help to maintain the carbonation.

VARIATIONS

Each of these can be added during step 1 or step 3 of the Basic Yeast-Pitched Soda.

GINGER SODA

1-inch piece fresh ginger root (double it up for more heat)

2 tablespoons fresh lemon juice

LEMON–LIME SODA

2 tablespoons fresh lemon juice

2 tablespoons fresh lime juice

MOJITO SODA

2 tablespoons fresh lime juice

10 fresh mint leaves

PIÑA COLADA SODA

3 tablespoons pineapple juice

2 tablespoons coconut milk

1 tablespoon fresh lime juice

BEET–CARROT–GINGER–APPLE SODA

1 tablespoon beet juice

1 tablespoon carrot juice

1-inch piece fresh ginger root

2 tablespoons apple juice or cider

KOMBUCHA

Known to many as "the elixir of life," kombucha, a beverage in the soda style that is made from tea and sugar, dominates the commercial market as one of the most popular nonalcoholic fermented drinks available. Over the past two decades, it has gone from an obscure alternative drink to a mainstream beverage seen in the hands of celebrities, athletes, and the general public. You don't have to go to a health food store to find kombucha anymore. Several national kombucha companies have worked hard to land it on the shelves of everyday grocery chains, transforming a dead drink aisle into a lively and healthful beverage section. That's why we refer to kombucha as the next yogurt: as more and more grocery chains add it to their product lines, kombucha is becoming as ubiquitous as its fermented predecessor. People who have memories from the 1950s will recall a time when yogurt was just a fledgling health food trend—an esoteric thing that was definitely not the norm.

We have become experts in the business and fermentation of kombucha through our company, Kombucha Brooklyn (KBBK), which we began back in 2009. From our viewpoint, it is not arbitrary that kombucha is the chosen one of the nonalcoholic or low-alcohol fermented beverages. Kombucha's substrate—sweetened, antioxidant-rich, all-natural tea—is, in and of itself, considered one of the most complex and health-supportive beverages ever to exist. In kombucha, this powerhouse beverage is supertransformed in multiple stages of fermentation by a handful of very different microbes, both yeast and bacteria. Somewhere between a mead, a lacto-ferment, and an acetic acid vinegar ferment, kombucha is a treasure trove of nutrition and fermentation. The acids formed in kombucha fermentation have an array of functions. From glucaric acid, a powerful agent that tones the liver, to butyric acid, which has been shown to nourish healthy gut cells and even subdue inflamed ones, these acids and others make up the brew's functional backbone and are up there on the list of why people flock to the drink. Additionally, kombucha is full of probiotics, whose virtues we have already discussed in the Introduction.

Kombucha is hardy, safe, and simple to make—just easy enough that we think this amazing drink is the best one for beginners to cut their teeth on. The process begins by steeping anything from the *Camellia sinensis* family, known throughout the world as "tea." Tea varietals can be of black, green, white, oolong, or pu-erh style. As long as it is from the *Camellia sinensis* family, it will contain the nutrients necessary for a flourishing kombucha colony. Next, a sweetener is added. Most of the kombucha cultures found worldwide are currently cultivated using cane sugar, but cultures that feed off other nutrients are available too, like "Jun," a culture that feeds off honey (our previous book, *Kombucha! The Amazing Probiotic Tea That Cleanses, Heals, Energizes, and Detoxifies*, covers this in detail).

kombucha SCOBYs

After the substrate is prepared and cooled, the kombucha culture, or SCOBY (Symbiotic Culture Of Bacteria and Yeast), is added. Kombucha SCOBYs, also known as "mothers," can be obtained in many places. Avoid dehydrated or frozen SCOBYs, which some companies sell. We have done the side-by-side comparison, and they just are not up to snuff. Our SCOBYs are the best we've ever

sampled, and you can buy one on our website. You can also get one from a kombucha-brewing friend.

Once you have one, you'll be able to make many, many more batches of kombucha, because each time you brew the drink, a new SCOBY will form in addition to the one you started with. Before long, you will have every neighbor, friend, and foe brewing kombucha with the offspring of your SCOBY.

But what exactly is it? A kombucha SCOBY is a cellulose patty that contains the microbes that ferment kombucha—yeast, lactic acid–forming bacteria, and acetic acid–forming bacteria. These microbes live symbiotically and construct more SCOBYs from the substrate. SCOBYs are curious artifacts that make passing kombucha culture around and down the line easy and fun. They are perfectly safe to play with, eat, or use to beautify your skin. If you are curious about the many uses of SCOBYs, check out our previous book!

The best way to make kombucha is to also add a bit of previously fermented kombucha to the substrate. It lowers the pH right off the bat and discourages any unwanted microbes from trying to take root in your brew. It also boosts the kombucha-specific microbial count!

Once your nutrients and culture are sitting in their fermentation vessel, tightly

We make a variety of vinegars in our home fermenting kitchen using kombucha SCOBYs, which have all the microbes needed to make excellent homemade vinegars from red wine, white wine, grape juice, beer, apple juice, and apple cider. These SCOBYs will produce vinegars while often forming a new SCOBY on the surface. The new SCOBY formed will likely not be able to make great kombucha out of sweet tea but may produce another round or two (or sometimes many more!) of vinegar.

Kombucha itself can be left to ferment well beyond the point when you'd like to tip up a glass of it; it will become its own unique vinegar that can be used in many recipes: as a sour mix in cocktails, a pan deglazer, or to add tartness to stir-fries. We have several cloth-covered half-gallon jars on the shelf at any given time, each a different substrate being turned into vinegar by a kombucha SCOBY. These jars will sit covered with a cloth for between one and six months, depending on the substrate and the temperature.

To start a vinegar ferment, take one to two cups of your chosen substrate, beer, for example, and add half a cup of fermented kombucha and a piece of kombucha SCOBY that is roughly the circumference of your jar (this recipe is easily scaled using these same proportions). A new SCOBY will form on the surface of your substrate, but it will take a good bit longer than it does in sweetened tea. You'll know when your vinegar is done because it will taste like . . .
vinegar! You can also use a pH strip to determine its exact acidity. Most people like their vinegar to be somewhere between a pH of 3 and 4. If you will use the vinegar for pickling projects, we recommend you bring it down to a pH of 4 for safety reasons. When your vinegar is finished, it can be stored for a year or more in a sealed container at room temperature, with or without the SCOBY.

cover the jar with a rubber band and cloth, allowing the brew to breathe while protecting it from fruit flies and other pests. Place the jar someplace it can sit undisturbed throughout the primary fermentation process at room temperature. Fermentation takes ten to fourteen days, depending on how you like it, with the results sweeter on the short side and tarter on the long side.

After your kombucha has undergone primary fermentation in its open-air vessel, you can take it in any of several different directions. Your choices will have a huge impact on the kombucha you will eventually drink. You can drink it straight from the fermentation vessel or bottle it, loosely capped, and put it in the fridge immediately. This will result in a delicious, tart, and soothingly still anytime beverage. Or you can bottle your kombucha and let it sit at room temperature—the bottle conditioning stage. This is how to obtain the effervescence that everyone is crazy about with kombucha.

A good kombucha fizz will be very much like champagne: small velvety bubbles that glide over your tongue. The rate at which your kombucha will develop those bubbles depends on the amount of sugar available in the bottle (either left over after primary fermentation or introduced before bottling through added flavoring or more sugar), the amount of yeast that makes it into the bottle, and the temperature at which the bottle conditioning is carried out. When kombucha is bottled with no additions, bubbles might take two to three weeks to form, depending on how much sugar remains at bottling. If you add fresh ingredients, though, you may have bubbles in as little as two days, depending again on sugar content. Be careful not to let your kombucha overferment in the bottle. Overfermentation will result in excessive bubbles and/or a drink that is too harshly acidic to enjoy.

If you bottle your kombucha in glass bottles, bottle some in a plastic bottle as well, to gauge the carbonation levels. As the fermentation progresses, the plastic bottle will get tight, then start bowing out as the pressure builds inside, giving you a good idea of how far along your kombucha is. This way you will not have to break the seal on the rest of your glass bottles to test your brew.

Bottle conditioning will continue in the refrigerator, although at a greatly reduced rate. If you will drink the kombucha within a week or so, put your bottles in the fridge when you think they are ready to drink. If you want to bottle condition the kombucha at a very slow pace, say a month or more, try placing your bottles in the refrigerator a day or so after bottling, similar to lagering beer. The results can be splendid and smooth. Of course, if you have a bum seal, opening your highly anticipated kombucha bottle after months of waiting can be a disappointment if you were hoping for smooth carbonation.

You can also mix fresh ingredients into your kombucha after primary fermentation—we highly encourage this. It will give your brew a unique twist without affecting the health of your kombucha culture. The possibilities here are endless. If your palate wants it, try it! We have been making kombucha for a long time, and the only thing we have found that doesn't go great with kombucha is celery. It's just a little too vegetal for our palates. We haven't tested them, but cruciferous vegetables, like broccoli, cauliflower, and cabbage, would be something to steer clear of, in our opinion. But who knows? If you want to give them a try, by all means! Let us know how it goes. Whatever you try, organics are always a wise choice.

Brewers can rest assured that if they start with a healthy, live SCOBY and use the right amount of pure ingredients along the way, a safe, delicious brew will await when they pop the cap.

✻   ✻   ✻   ✻   ✻   ✻   ✻   ✻

BASIC KOMBUCHA

Use any of the selected tea blends found on pages 137–139 for your kombucha.

Yield: 1 gallon

12 grams tea, loose or bagged

1 cup cane sugar

1 cup starter liquid (already-brewed kombucha)

1 SCOBY

Vessel: 1-gallon wide-mouth jar or ceramic crock with cloth cover

Duration: 10 to 14 days

1. Bring 1 quart of water to boil in a large pot over high heat.

2. Turn off the heat and add the tea. Let steep for 20 minutes, stirring and agitating the tea every 5 minutes.

3. Add 2 quarts of cool water to the brewing vessel. It is imperative that the water be cool. When the hot tea is added in the next step, it will bring the temperature down enough for it to be safe for the brew vessel and the kombucha culture.

4. Add the steeped tea to your vessel already containing cool water, using a strainer to remove the tea leaves, or remove the tea bags.

5. Add the sugar to the cooled tea and mix thoroughly.

6. Add the starter liquid and SCOBY to the cool, sweet tea.

7. Add more cool water to bring the volume to 1 gallon.

8. Cover with a tightly knit cloth and seal with a rubber band. Let sit for 10 to 14 days at room temperature.

9. Most people prefer their primary kombucha fermentation to be halted when the brew is tart with a nice balance of sweetness. Use a clean sample thief (see page 52) to dip into the brew and test it at any time If you don't have a sample thief, you can use a clean spoon or teacup to push down the SCOBY and retrieve a sample. Like other ferments, the kombucha is perfectly healthy and safe to drink at any time during fermentation.

10. When you have determined that your kombucha is finished, transfer all but 1 cup of kombucha directly into bottles or into a separate pot (you can flavor individual bottles or the entire batch at once). Put the reserved cup of kombucha and the new SCOBY into a tightly sealed container and store in the refrigerator to use in the next batch. You can store and reuse, discard, compost, donate, or eat the other, older SCOBY.

11. After flavoring your kombucha as desired (see "Other Suggested Additions for Bottle Conditioning," page 140), seal the bottles and allow them to sit at room temperature for 3 days to gain carbonation through bottle conditioning. If you do not want further fermentation and carbonation, skip this step and transfer the kombucha bottles directly to the refrigerator. If you let your kombucha bottles condition, when finished put them in the refrigerator. They will continue to ferment slowly in the refrigerator. After about one month, the flavor will start to change.

Kombucha begins as sweet tea. As the fermentation progresses, the brew will become more and more tart. The SCOBY will also grow thicker along the way and can generally be used a visual gauge of how far along your brew is.

Dry Apple Cider, page 149

Soy Sauce–Brined Japanese Pickle, page 78

Asian Pear Curried Kimchi, page 74

Sauerkraut, Apple, and Fennel Salad with Walnuts, page 70

Basic Beet Kvass, page 127

Various fermented vegetables, page 59

Sour Cherry Wine, page 158

Basic Water Kefir (with blueberries), page 142

Asian Pear Curried Kimchi, page 74

Lacto-Fermented Giardiniera, page 77

Tempeh, page 102

The Tempehst's Orange-Ginger Tempeh over Coconut Rice, page 103

Honey Amaro, page 178

Ginger Beer, page 174

Kombucha tea blends

Our Basic Kombucha recipe can be made with a variety of different teas or tea blends. The blend that we use in all KBBK's Kombucha Home Brew Kits is called our Straight-Up Blend. This blend gives the SCOBY all the nutrients it craves, and it delivers all the flavor that will keep you brewing for more. Black tea provides a high level of nitrogen for new SCOBY growth, green tea nutrients tend to speed up the fermentation process, and white tea brings a delicious fruity floral taste to tie

them all together. It makes a great stand-alone kombucha and is also the perfect base for mixing flavors into after primary fermentation. Remember, just like the other ferments covered in this book, using high-quality ingredients is the foundation of a great ferment. For more insight, tips, and suggestions about tea blending for kombucha, visit our website at www.kombuchabk.com.

KBBK'S STRAIGHT-UP TEA BLEND

Yield: 12 grams (enough tea blend for 1 Basic Kombucha recipe of 1 gallon)

4 grams Yunnan black tea

4 grams Dragonwell green tea

4 grams White Peony tea

1. Weigh out each tea.

2. Mix together for brewing.

3. Steep the tea blend for 20 minutes, agitating every 5 minutes.

We have been very successful blending all sorts of tea styles in the same equal proportions that we use in the Straight-Up recipe. Don't be afraid to play around with blending different tea styles. You can use one tea type to enhance and augment another in flavor and nutrition. Other teas we suggest for creating various combinations for brewing kombucha are:

Wild Jungle green pu-erh

Imperial pu-erh

Tieguanyin oolong

Phoenix Mountain oolong

Honey Orchid black

Golden Monkey black

Jasmine green

Silver Needle white

Kombucha botanical blends

Once you master tea blending for kombucha, you can dive into the art of blending herbs and spices to use as a substrate along with tea. Using different botanicals to make kombucha can yield complex brews with distinctive flavors and health characteristics. Be careful, though. The ingredients you use as the substrate are the nutrients that feed the kombucha SCOBY. If you start to use different nutrients along with your tea, you may in fact change the microbial fingerprint of your SCOBY. This means that your SCOBY

may or may not maintain its vibrancy and resiliency. This is why we always recommend having a backup storage of your basic tea mother culture along with some basic tea kombucha as a starter, known as a SCOBY hotel. This way, if you ever find that the original health and vigor of your culture has been compromised by being tossed into various experiments, you can always revert to the original.

A SCOBY hotel is essentially a jar full of old SCOBYs bathed in kombucha and left covered in your fridge. This way, you can always go back to your original robust strain. Because of the very low pH of this long-fermenting concoction (it is actually kombucha vinegar; see sidebar about vinegars, page 133), it should resist mold growth for a very long time, especially in the refrigerator.

To get you started brewing with botanicals in addition to your tea, here is one of our favorite recipes, aptly named after our first son, Rider, who was the easiest baby in the world.

E-Z RIDER

Use one recipe of E-Z Rider in place of the 12 grams loose tea in the Basic Kombucha recipe. It will yield a gallon of kombucha very reminiscent of root beer. Its earthy notes are balanced by a bounty of fruitiness, where you'll find apples, pears, and Mandarin oranges dancing on the palate.

Yield: 24 grams

8 grams Indian sarsaparilla

8 grams sassafras

Pinch of birch bark

6 grams Wild Jungle Green pu-erh

1. Mix the ingredients and store them in an airtight jar until use. Tea blend will keep for a year before becoming stale. You can scale this recipe up and make enough for several rounds in advance!

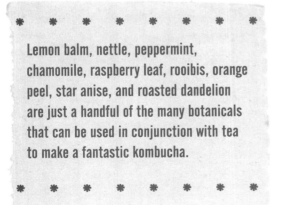

Lemon balm, nettle, peppermint, chamomile, raspberry leaf, rooibis, orange peel, star anise, and roasted dandelion are just a handful of the many botanicals that can be used in conjunction with tea to make a fantastic kombucha.

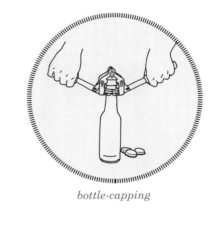

bottle-capping

Kombucha flavoring blends

In our experiments with flavoring during bottle conditioning, we have come across some brilliant synergistic ingredients. Here are a few of our favorite blends of juices, herbs, and whole fruit to add upon bottling.

WATERMELLOW

Yield: 16 ounces

4 ounces watermelon juice

½ ounce lime juice

1. Combine watermelon juice and lemon juice with enough kombucha to fill one 16-ounce bottle.

2. Tightly seal cap and leave at room temperature for 2 days.

3. Transfer to the refrigerator and consume within 3 months.

* * * * * * * *

LEMON GINGER

Yield: 16 ounces

1 ounce lemon juice

1 ounce ginger juice

1. Combine lemon juice and ginger juice with enough kombucha to fill one 16-ounce bottle.

2. Tightly seal cap and leave at room temperature for 4 days.

3. Transfer to the refrigerator and consume within 6 months.

* * * * * * * *

BIG APPLE MINT

Yield: 16 ounces

4 ounces apple cider

3 fresh mint leaves

1. Combine apple cider and mint leaves with enough kombucha to fill one 16-ounce bottle.

2. Add mint leaves to bottle.

3. Tightly seal cap and leave at room temperature for 4 days.

4. Transfer to the refrigerator and consume within 6 months.

OTHER SUGGESTED ADDITIONS FOR BOTTLE CONDITIONING

Remember to consider the sugar and yeast content of any additions you plan to blend into kombucha before bottling. We have found that some ingredients that you wouldn't think are high in sugar, like chia seeds, actually pack a huge punch with complex sugars that microbes make short work of. As chia seeds also carry their own host of yeasts, kombuchas bottle-conditioned with them carbonate very quickly. When adding ingredients like chia, be sure to put the bottles in the fridge after a very short stay at room temperature. Also, be sure to slowly open your bottles over the sink!

Fruit juices

Lemon	Apple	Grapefruit
Grape	Watermelon	

Fruit—chopped, fresh, or dried

Strawberry	Blueberry	Pear
Apple	Cantaloupe	

Herbs

Mint	Rosemary	Oregano

Roots

Ginger	Turmeric	Garlic

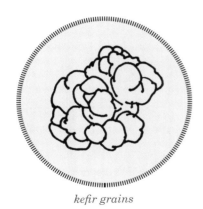

kefir grains

KEFIR

A close relative of kombucha, kefir is a quick, easy, and delicious ferment to prepare. There are two distinct styles of kefir and they each feed on different substrates: dairy kefir and water kefir. Similar to kombucha, both styles of kefir form SCOBYs during fermentation. Instead of forming a patty on the surface of the brew, however, they form little granular balls that settle on the bottom of your brew or dance around within the liquid throughout fermentation. Like kombucha SCOBYs, kefir SCOBYs (also known as kefir grains) multiply with each brew, giving you a lifelong supply. The primary fermentation process for kefir takes only twenty-four to forty-eight hours before the delicate and refreshing ferment is ready to drink.

The basic substrate of water kefir is some form of sugar in a water solution. Most recipes use plain white sugar and include the addition of another ingredient such as dried fruit—like raisins or figs. We find that the addition of dried fruit bumps up the flavor profile and results in a more satisfying beverage. We also have found that mineral-rich sugars like Rapadura, Sucanat, or Demerara work very well in this ferment. The addition of lemon juice prior to fermentation adds a spark of floral acidity and lowers the pH, ensuring a safe environment for the grains to ferment and multiply. Once fermented, water kefir can be bottled and undergo bottle conditioning to carbonate and further refine the flavor.

Dairy kefir, like the name so aptly suggests, feeds on milk. We have fermented all varieties of milk with our dairy grains, from low-fat milk to heavy cream, goat's milk to coconut milk. They all produce their own unique variety of kefir. For more on this, flip back to Chapter 4: Dairy Lacto-Fermentation. Keep in mind that your culture will adapt to what it is exposed to, so it may take a few rounds of brewing to get a good-flavored, quick-fermenting coconut milk kefir using grains that were formerly trained to low-fat milk, for example. But keep at it, and usually the grains will eventually adapt. Unlike water kefir, which needs bottle conditioning to develop effervescence, dairy kefir usually traps more of the carbon dioxide produced during primary fermentation even when only loosely capped. Perhaps this is due to the liquid's increased viscosity. If you desire even further carbonation, you can bottle condition dairy kefir as well.

Either type of kefir can be fermented in a closed or open environment. We like to cover the top of our jar loosely during primary fermentation with cloth or a loose lid, allowing for nice oxygen flow to the yeasts in the culture. Once fermented, the kefir will be strained to remove and reserve the grains. For water kefir, use a very fine mesh strainer and pour gently so you do not disturb the outer surface of the grains. For dairy kefir grains, we find it easier to fish them out with a clean regular or slotted spoon. Whatever you do, *never, ever rinse your dairy or water kefir grains with water*. This is nonnegotiable. If you wash them with water, they will not only dissolve to some degree but also lose their protective layer coating the surface of the grains. The next time you try to ferment with them, the ferment will go exceptionally fast and be hard to control. You can bring rinsed grains back from the brink, as long as the damage isn't too extensive. But it is a pain, wastes ingredients and energy, and definitely disrupts your fermenting flow. Either store your grains refrigerated, covered with some already-made kefir in a tightly sealed jar, or start your next batch immediately.

One great thing about kefir is that it is a fast ferment. In our house, we go through kefir crazes a couple of times per year, where every day we brew enough for the family to drink the next day. Eventually, we get a little over-kefired and we retire our grains to the compost. When the craze hits again, we ask a friend for some extra grains and get the jar rolling again! We have friends who have been brewing from the same grains for years. Every fermenting kitchen has its flow.

The best way to obtain kefir grains is from someone you know. They will be able to provide you with information on how the grains perform, what they have been fed, etc. If you can't find grains this way, try Gem Cultures; we have tried several providers of kefir grains and have found their strain to be very robust.

✳ ✳ ✳ ✳ ✳ ✳ ✳ ✳

BASIC WATER KEFIR

This recipe produces a semisweet lemony brew that is both refreshing and energizing. It can be tweaked in many ways to add different flavor profiles. As the fermentation process gets underway, the grains will get carried away by the CO_2 forming in the liquid and dance around in your brew vessel. For this reason, we love brewing in glass to watch the dance unfold. It's a magical tango of fermentation awesomeness.

Yield: 1 gallon

2 tablespoons sugar (ideally unrefined and hence mineral-rich)

12 goji berries

2 teaspoons lemon juice

3-inch lemon rind

2 tablespoons kefir grains

Vessel: 1-gallon glass jar with lid or cloth cover
Duration: 24 to 48 hours

1. Warm ¼ cup of water in a saucepan over medium heat.

2. Add sugar and stir to dissolve.

3. Add the sugar mixture and ½ gallon of cool water to the vessel.

4. Add goji berries, lemon juice, and lemon rind.

5. Make sure the liquid has cooled to around room temperature, then add the kefir grains.

6. Cover and let sit for 24 to 48 hours at room temperature (74 to 78°F), depending on the specifics of your setup (temperature, airflow, and so on) and how acidic you like your brew.

7. Remove the grains by passing the kefir through a fine-mesh strainer or fishing them out with a long spoon. Do not rinse them in water! Store the grains in a sealed container in the refrigerator, covered in kefir, or use them immediately in your next batch.

8. At this point, you can bottle condition your water kefir straight or with the addition of flavoring agents such as herbs or dried fruit. We have also had success transferring the fruit from primary fermentation into the bottles for bottle conditioning. Depending on the sugar content and microbe count, the water kefir will condition to a good level of effervescence in 1 to 4 days at room temperature. Transfer bottles to the fridge, where they will keep for up to 1 month. After that, kefir starts to taste yeasty.

Here are a few awesome additions for your Basic Water Kefir. These are so good, we rarely stray from them. Use them alone or in concert with one another. You can add these during primary fermentation or at bottling time for a lively bottle of kefir.

White figs

Mango chunks

Fresh thyme

Fresh blueberries

Goji berries

BASIC DAIRY KEFIR

Dairy kefir is remarkably refreshing with light effervescence and tang. Dairy milk has innate sugar in the form of lactose. Even lactose-free milks have sugars in a broken-down form. Because of this, there is no need to add additional sugar to milk prior to fermentation. We make our kefir using pure milk and add our flavorings prior to serving, keeping our options open, and the fruits, nuts, or grains that we add maintain their crispness.

Yield: 1 quart

4 cups milk (see Chapter 4: Dairy Lacto-Fermentation for notes about various milks)

2 tablespoons kefir grains

Vessel: 1-quart jar with screw-top lid
Duration: 24 to 48 hours

1. Pour your milk of choice into a 1-quart jar.

2. Add the kefir grains and close the lid loosely.

3. Set aside at room temperature for 24 hours.

4. Give the jar a slight jiggle. The kefir should be more viscous than the fresh milk you began with. Dip a clean spoon in and give it a taste. When it has sufficient effervescence and acidity, it is ready to drink!

5. Use a clean spoon to remove the grains from the ferment. Store the grains in a sealed container in the refrigerator, covered in kefir for up to a week, or use them immediately in your next batch.

6. Seal the lid on your kefir and store in the refrigerator. Your kefir will continue to ferment slowly in the fridge, and the whey will start to pool on the surface. Shake to mix the whey back into the kefir. It will keep up to 3 weeks in refrigeration.

As with the viili and the yogurt in Part II: Eat, kefir can also be strained through cheesecloth to change its consistency— from a thicker, sour cream-like consistency all the way to a dense, goat cheese-like consistency. The leftover whey can be used to start bread kvass or other lacto-ferments.

If dairy is not your thing, dairy kefir grains are usually easily trained to a variety of nut, seed, and grain milks. To do this, take your grains and bathe them in a few successive baths of the new milk, each time for 8 hours. After this, start a batch of kefir using your transformed grains in the new milk type. It may take a few rounds to get them performing optimally, but in a week or so, you should have fast-fermenting kefir grains trained to your milk of choice.

chapter 7

~ HARD CIDER ~

A classic in many households around the world, cider is most commonly known as a nonalcoholic—or more accurately, a low-alcohol—drink made from the juice of apples or other orchard fruit. When this delicious staple is allowed to ferment, the result is hard cider, an alcoholic treat served bubbly or still. For centuries, hard cider has been made simply by collecting apples, both from the tree and off the surrounding ground, crushing them whole, and then fermenting the naturally inoculated juice. Wild yeasts on the outside of the fruit make this fermentation possible, and the finished product is dry, tart, and deliciously low in alcohol, usually around 3 to 5 percent. The drink is easy to make and good to drink year-round. Another way to prepare it is by juicing the apples, which frees up lots and lots of sugar for immediate access, and pitching in a higher volume of yeast. This makes for a fast ferment that can be reproduced over and over again with the same results.

In the Normandy region of France—a classic region for hard cider, where we were first introduced to farmhouse cider-making—the tradition goes back to the sixteenth century. Each farm's own technique and recipe yields a unique cider that can be starkly different from even the farms directly surrounding it. Normandy farmhouse ciders are consumed throughout the year and used as bartering currency among locals. Farms trade their own unique apple tree grafts along with representative bottles of cider during Easter celebrations, which coincide with the spring growing season. These ciders are almost always made in the traditional way—using native yeasts—and they tend to be delectably dry. Although the conditions in which many homemade farm ciders in Normandy would appear rough, with such a high degree of pride and attention to detail, the results are complex, fine, and delicious hard ciders. Most of the fermentation and bottling work is strategically planned and carried out around the time of a waning moon, early in the morning at first light. A romantic idea, though it is hard to challenge after sipping a glass of fresh Normandy farmhouse cider.

To make hard cider using whole apples, you first need to select and gather your apples. Very damaged or under-ripened apples need to be discarded from the bunch, as they create displeasing and dull acid notes. Overripe apples are wonderful in this ferment as they contribute more sugar and soft, abundant floral notes. Once picked, the apples need to be washed thoroughly with water. Next, the apples are crushed and their juices captured. During this step, the juice, tannin, pectin, and yeast are gathered. In a traditional apple press, two wooden plates moved by a crank or wheel smash the apples together. A container below the press collects the juice that issues forth. It is either left to sit out in the open for 12 hours, capturing more environmental yeast, or transferred directly into the fermentation vessel. In the home fermenting kitchen, you can juice apples yourself using a juicer, or you can start with fresh nonalcoholic apple cider that you purchase from a farm stand or grocery store.

The traditional primary fermentation vessel is a huge wooden cask. In the home fermenting kitchen, a smaller fermentation vessel—such as a fermentation bucket or a glass jug—with an air lock is sufficient. It is easiest to pitch a culture of cider yeast into your juice. We have used English cider yeast, American cider yeast, champagne yeast, and ale yeast to ferment cider, all with great success; each has its own unique qualities. You will start to see activity from the yeast after the juice has fermented for a couple of days at a cool temperature (60 to 70°F).

carboy with air lock

Once primary fermentation has slowed and bubbles are seen in your air lock only once every two minutes or so, the liquid is transferred to another vessel, using a racking cane to leave behind the lees for secondary fermentation. Racking at this point is important because during secondary fermentation, you don't want the remaining yeast to exhaust the sugar and other nutrients and then eat the dead yeast cells; this would result in an undrinkable cider with off flavors. Secondary fermentation usually happens in a glass carboy sealed tightly with an air lock to keep any additional yeast, bacteria, or oxygen from entering the brew. This stage can take up to two months, depending on the temperature.

When air bubbles stop presenting in the air lock, the cider is then transferred to bottles and sealed. Bottle conditioning without any further addition of sugar or yeast at a cool temperature for a few months will round out the flavors and yield a delicious, bubbly brew. Ciders are best when fermented at lower temperatures; the low to mid sixties are perfect.

Using pasteurized juice and adding yeast, rather than using the wild yeasts from apples in the field, may yield a faster result, higher alcohol level, and often a cleaner, more reproducible taste. The overall sweetness of cider is dependent on the amount of sugar and yeast and how long you let the fermentation progress. We once were told that if we wanted a perfect cider we would need to wait at least a year from start to finish. However, we have found that we get excellent cider ringing in at an alcohol level of 4 to 5 percent in just under two months.

❋   ❋   ❋   ❋   ❋   ❋   ❋   ❋

DRY APPLE CIDER

Yield: 1 gallon

1 gallon pasteurized apple cider

¼ tube liquid English cider yeast

1 teaspoon yeast nutrient

1 teaspoon acid blend

½ teaspoon pectic enzyme

Pinch of tannin

Vessel: Two 1-gallon glass jugs
Duration: 3 to 6 weeks

1. Measure ½ cup of cider into a sanitized 1-quart jar. Pour the yeast in, cover tightly with a clean lid, and shake vigorously. Allow this yeast starter to stand in a warm environment around 78°F until bubbly, about 1 hour.

2. Pour the rest of the apple cider into a sanitized 1-gallon jug. Add the yeast starter, yeast nutrient, acid blend, pectic enzyme, and tannin. Stir the mixture well.

3. Seal the jug with a sanitized bung and air lock and allow to stand at room temperature. Over the next 48 hours, there will be active fermentation—bubbles will be visible in the air lock.

4. Let the cider ferment, undisturbed, for no less than 3 days and up to 7 days. Fermentation activity will slow down, and the sediment should settle at the bottom of the jug.

5. Sanitize a racking cane and tip and another 1-gallon jug. Siphon the hard cider into the new clean jug, leaving all sediment behind in the original jug. Seal with a sanitized bung and air lock. Allow the cider to sit for 2 weeks in a cool and dark place.

6. After 2 weeks, it's time to bottle. Sanitize your bottles and their caps, then siphon the cider into them using a sanitized racking cane and tip, again leaving behind any sediment. Cap and label the bottles and allow them to sit at least 1 month at a cool temperature before drinking. The cider will keep for up to a year stored at cellar temperatures and is best enjoyed chilled.

* * * * * * * *

PEAR-APPLE HARD CIDER

Yield: 1 gallon

12 cups pasteurized pear cider

1 packet champagne yeast

4 cups pasteurized apple cider

1 teaspoon yeast nutrient

½ teaspoon pectic enzyme

1 teaspoon acid blend

Pinch of tannin

24 raisins

Vessel: Two 1-gallon glass jugs

Duration: 3 to 6 weeks

1. Measure ½ cup of pear cider into a sanitized 1-quart jar. Pour the yeast in, cover tightly with a clean lid, and shake vigorously. Allow the yeast starter to stand on a heat mat until bubbly.

2. Pour the rest of the pear and apple ciders into a sanitized 1-gallon jug. Add the yeast starter, yeast nutrient, pectic enzyme, acid blend, and tannin. Stir the mixture well. Seal the jug with a sanitized bung and air lock. Over the next 48 hours, there should be active fermentation—you will see bubbles in the air lock.

3. Let the cider ferment, undisturbed, no less than 3 days, and up to 7 days. Fermentation activity should slow down, and the sediment should settle at the bottom of the jug.

4. Sanitize a racking cane and tip and another 1-gallon jug. Siphon the hard cider into the new jug, leaving all sediment behind in the original jug. Seal with a sanitized bung and air lock. Allow the cider to sit in secondary fermentation for 2 weeks in a cool and dark place.

5. After 2 weeks, it's time to bottle. Sanitize your bottles and their caps, then siphon the cider into them using a sanitized racking cane and tip, again leaving behind any sediment. Drop in 6 raisins per 32-ounce bottle, then cap them. Label your bottles and allow to bottle condition for at least 1 month before drinking. The cider will keep for up to a year stored at cellar temperatures and is best enjoyed chilled.

chapter 8

∾ WINE ∾

"Wine is the most healthful and most hygienic of beverages."
—LOUIS PASTEUR

"his lips drink water but his heart drinks wine"
—E. E. CUMMINGS

Wine made from fruit is one of the oldest and most culturally significant of the fermented beverages. Today, wine remains a part of every meal in many cultures worldwide. The most commonly known variety of wine is made from grapes from the species known as *Vitis vinifera*. These grapes are the only known fruit to have the perfect spectrum of naturally occurring sugars and yeasts to make high-alcohol wine without any additions. These grapes also are the only fruit that has the highly specific balance of tannins and acids to result in what we all know wine to be: bottled poetry.

When Jessica was growing up, her father owned and operated a small Riesling vineyard. Eric holds a certificate from the International Wine Center. We have no lack of love for wine in our home fermenting kitchen. In fact, we love it so much, we don't generally make it ourselves. We leave it to the families and entrepreneurs who dedicate their working life to perfecting it. Most of the wines we drink come from the Old World, where serious winemaking goes back hundreds of years. These wines are made using natural, local traditions passed down from winemaker to winemaker, resulting in wines that cannot be replicated elsewhere. The soil, air quality, light quality, and water components specific to a winemaking region all play a role in the qualities of the grapes that are picked. In the hands of a dedicated winemaker, the heart and soul of distinctive wines are forged. Luckily, a wide range of exquisite wines can be made from other fruits.

In addition to grapes, wines can be made with all sorts of fruits, vegetables, and even nut substrates. All you have to do is pitch in a wine yeast and, perhaps, balance the flavor profile with the addition of an acid blend or tannins. After you've selected your primary ingredient, the first step in making wine is to make a must. Wine must is the mash you get after crushing and/or juicing fruit. The must is then inoculated with yeast and allowed to ferment in primary fermentation for a number of weeks before the liquid is racked to another vessel for secondary fermentation. Wines generally take longer to make than other drinkable ferments and typically yield higher amounts of alcohol. They are also sensitive to undesirable bacterial contamination. For this reason, it is essential to keep your environment, hardware, and hands clean and sanitized throughout the entire process with brew grade cleanser (PBW) and sanitizer (StarSan).

Fresh ingredients are usually the best choice when making wine, but for many this is not possible. Frozen fruit will work just fine in these recipes and, in some cases, frozen is better (see Chapter 2: The Fermenter's Pantry). In order to make sure you are not introducing unwanted contaminants to your fermentation, use Campden tablets to sterilize your fruit after making a mash. Campden tablets release a small amount of sulfur gas into the mash, making it a sterilized "blank slate" ready to be inoculated with a single strain of yeast. Be careful not to add your yeast during

If you have a hankering to make wine using *Vitis vinifera,* there are many print resources available. If you find a recipe that you think might change our mind about homemade wines, feel free to send it to us! Or better yet, bring some to or shop outside Woodstock, NY.

this step, as the sulfur will kill the yeast!

You can choose from a number of yeasts when you are making wine. Try to find a yeast strain that matches the style you are trying to get. Champagne yeast is our go-to variety for light, bright fruit like peaches, pineapple, or citrus. For darker fruit like cherries, strawberries, and blueberries, red wine yeasts are a better choice.

Wine can be bottled in almost any bottle that you might have in your pantry, but the traditional choice is a 750-milliliter long-necked bottle sealed with a cork. These bottles will age well and make a dramatic presentation when you serve your brew to your new best friends.

* * * * * * * *

BLACKBERRY WINE

Yield: 1 gallon

14 cups filtered water

4½ cups organic cane sugar

4⅓ pounds fresh organic blackberries, washed

1 Campden tablet

1 pack Montrachet dry wine yeast

2 teaspoons yeast nutrient

2 teaspoons acid blend

½ teaspoon pectic enzyme

¼ teaspoon tannin

Vessel: 1-gallon glass jar with lid and 1-gallon glass carboy or jug

Duration: 6 to 8 weeks

1. Prepare a 1-gallon wide-mouth jar and its lid by drilling a small hole in the lid and inserting a rubber O-ring into the hole. Sanitize the jug, its lid, an air lock, mesh bag, and a spoon.

2. Put the water in a stockpot set over medium-high heat. When the water begins to simmer, add the sugar and stir until it dissolves. Remove the pot from the heat, and allow the water to cool the water to room temperature.

3. Pour the sugar water into the sanitized jar. Secure the berries in a mesh bag, drop the bag into the sugar water, and with clean hands, squeeze the bag to release as much juice as possible from the berries. Leaving the bag of fruit in the jar, crush the Campden tablet into a fine powder, stir it into the mixture, put on the lid with the

* * * * * * * *

Don't get discouraged if your first attempt does not go as planned and you wind up with a vinegar. Try again and take extra special care in keeping your environment clean every step of the way, paying special attention to common points of contamination, like touching your hair, clothing, cell phones, or sink handles.

* * * * * * * *

air lock, and let it sit for 24 hours. This will sterilize the fruit.

4. After the fruit is sterilized, prepare a yeast starter. Sanitize a 1-cup measure, a 1-quart glass jar, and a stirring spoon. Measure out 1 cup of the fruity liquid and pour it into the jar. Pour the yeast over the juice, cover the jar with plastic wrap, and secure with a rubber band. Shake the jar and place it on a heat mat for at least 30 minutes. The mixture should become foamy and the plastic wrap will bulge when the yeast starter is ready.

5. Pour the yeast starter into the jar of berry juice. Also add the yeast nutrient, acid blend, pectic enzyme, and tannin. Stir vigorously for 15 seconds to aerate the liquid. Put the lid with the air lock back on. You should see activity in the air lock or on the surface of the liquid within 48 hours.

6. Let the wine ferment for 1 week at room temperature. Sanitize a 1-gallon carboy or jug, a rubber bung, an air lock, a strainer, a funnel, a flour sack towel or cheesecloth, and a long-handled spoon. Pull the bag of fruit out of the liquid with clean sanitized hands and squeeze it to get as much liquid out as possible.

7. Line the funnel with the cloth and put it in the mouth of the new jug. Slowly pour the wine through the funnel into the jug, using the spoon to help the liquid through the cheesecloth. Seal the jug with the bung and insert the air lock.

8. Let the wine sit for about 4 weeks in a cool, dark place. After 4 weeks, fermentation should have slowed way down; if no bubbles move through the air lock in a 2-minute interval, it is time to bottle.

9. Sanitize bottles, their caps, a stockpot, a siphon hose, a racking cane, and its tip. Siphon the wine into the stockpot, leaving the sediment behind. Then siphon the wine into the bottles, insuring that you leave more of the sediment behind, and put on the caps. It's helpful to label the bottles with the date.

10. Bottle condition in a cool, dark place for 2 weeks to 1 year. Serve the wine chilled or at room temperature.

✳   ✳   ✳   ✳   ✳   ✳   ✳   ✳

FROZEN BLUEBERRY WINE
Yield: 1 gallon

14 cups filtered water

4½ cups organic cane sugar

4⅓ pounds frozen organic blueberries

1 Campden tablet

1 pack Pasteur Red wine yeast

2 teaspoons yeast nutrient

2 teaspoons acid blend

½ teaspoon pectic enzyme

¼ teaspoon tannin

Vessel: 1-gallon glass jar with a lid and 1-gallon glass carboy or jug outfitted with an airlock

Duration: 6 to 8 weeks

1. Prepare a 1-gallon wide-mouth jar and its lid by drilling a small hole in the lid and inserting a rubber O-ring into the hole. Sanitize the jar, its lid, an air lock, mesh bag, and a spoon.

2. Put the water in a stockpot set over medium-high heat. When the water begins to simmer, add the sugar and stir until it dissolves. Remove the pot from the heat, and allow the water to cool to room temperature.

3. Pour the sugar water into the sanitized jar. Secure the berries in a mesh bag, drop the bag into the sugar water, and with clean hands, squeeze the bag to release the juices. Leaving the bag of fruit in the jar, crush the Campden tablet into a fine powder, stir it into the mixture, put on the lid with the air lock, and let it sit for 24 hours. This will sterilize the fruit.

4. After the fruit is sterilized, prepare a yeast starter. Sanitize a 1-cup measure, a 1-quart glass jar, and a stirring spoon. Measure out 1 cup of the fruity liquid, and pour it into the jar. Pour the yeast over the juice, cover the jar with plastic wrap, and secure with a rubber band. Shake the jar and place it on a heat mat for at least 30 minutes. The mixture should become foamy and the plastic wrap will bulge when the yeast starter is ready.

5. Pour the yeast starter into the jar of berry juice. Add the yeast nutrient, acid blend, pectic enzyme, and tannin. Stir vig-orously for 15 seconds to aerate the liquid. Put the lid with the air lock back on. You should see activity in the air lock and on the surface of the liquid within 48 hours.

6. Let the wine ferment for 1 week at room temperature. Sanitize a 1-gallon carboy or jug, a rubber bung, an air lock, a strainer, a funnel, a flour sack towel or cheesecloth, and a long-handled spoon. Pull the bag of fruit out of the liquid with clean sanitized hands and squeeze out the liquid.

7. Line the funnel with the cloth and put it in the mouth of the new jug. Slowly pour the wine through the funnel into the jug, using the spoon to help the liquid through the cheesecloth. Seal the jug with the bung and insert the air lock.

8. Let the wine sit for about 4 to 6 weeks in a cool, dark place. If no bubbles move through the air lock in a 2-minute interval, it is time to bottle.

9. Sanitize bottles, their caps, a stockpot, a siphon hose, a racking cane, and its tip. Siphon the wine into the stockpot, leaving the sediment behind. Then siphon the wine into the bottle, insuring that you leave all the sediment behind, and put on the caps.

10. Bottle condition in a cool, dark place for 2 weeks to 1 year. Serve the wine chilled or at room temperature.

* * * * * * * *

SOUR CHERRY WINE

Yield: 1 gallon

1 gallon sour cherry juice

1 pack Pasteur Red wine yeast

2 teaspoons yeast nutrient

½ teaspoon pectic enzyme

¼ teaspoon tannin

25 raisins (or 5 teaspoons honey, sugar, or maple syrup)

Vessel: Two 1-gallon glass jugs

Duration: 6 to 8 weeks

1. Sanitize a 1-gallon jug, a rubber bung, and an air lock. Pour 15 of the cups of the cherry juice into the jug.

2. Sanitize a 1-cup measure, a 1-quart glass jar with lid and a stirring spoon. Put the remaining cup of juice into the quart jar. Pour the yeast over the juice, cover the jar tightly with the lid, and shake the jar tightly with lid and shake the jar vigorously. Place the jar in a warm environment for at least 30 minutes. The mixture should become foamy when the yeast starter is ready.

3. Pour the yeast starter into the jug of juice. Also add the yeast nutrient, pectic enzyme, and tannin. Stir vigorously for 15 seconds to aerate the liquid. Seal the jug with the bung and air lock. You should see activity in the air lock and on the surface of the liquid within 48 hours. Let the wine ferment for 1 week.

4. Sanitize another 1-gallon jug, a siphon hose, a racking cane, and its tip, a bung, and an air lock. Transfer the wine into the new jug, leaving the sediment behind. Seal the jug with the bung and the air lock.

5. Let the wine sit for about 4 weeks in a cool, dark place. If no bubbles pass through the air lock in a 2-minute interval, it is time to bottle.

6. Sanitize bottles, their caps, a stockpot, a siphon hose, a racking cane, and its tip. Put 5 raisins (or 1 teaspoon of honey, sugar, or maple syrup) in each bottle. Then siphon the wine into the stockpot, leaving the sediment behind. Siphon the wine into the bottles, insuring that you leave behind all the sediment, and put on the caps. It's helpful to label the bottles with the date.

7. Bottle condition in a cool, dark place for 2 weeks to 1 year. Serve the wine chilled or at room temperature, and expect a delightful amount of carbonation.

chapter 9

∽ BEER ∾

"Beer is the proof that God loves us and wants us to be happy."
—BENJAMIN FRANKLIN

Most Western people think of beer as a barley- or wheat-based ferment, made bitter and preserved with hops, usually bearing an alcohol content between 4 and 6 percent ABV. Golden and bubbly, barley beers are thought to have originated in Mesopotamia around the fifth millennium BCE. Ale, lager, Pilsner, Hefeweizen, Weizenbock, stout, porter, and many more beer styles lay claim to this lineage and have our modern images of beer.

Around the same time that folks in Mesopotamia were first enjoying the fruits of their newly established agricultural community, people in other civilizations around the globe were developing similar farming and brewing technologies using grains and starchy tubers that were native to their own lands. In the Asian Himalayas, rice, barley, and millet were used to make a sweet and silky beer called *chhaang*. Maize, potatoes, and yucca were the base for *chicha* in the stepped-terrace agriculture program that was in full swing in the Americas. Still other beer-like beverage recipes have been created using an assortment of other starchy ingredients like the cores of pineapples or ginger roots. Once you widen your vision of what beer can be, you'll be a global citizen clinking glasses with your ancestors. Low in alcohol, high in flavor, and oh so refreshing, beer is indeed a gift from the gods.

BARLEY BEER

A good pint of barley suds will nourish, soften, and make anyone's day. An astonishing number of breweries in America, Europe, and around the world are brewing a number of classic barley beer styles. These classics have deep roots in ancient Mesopotamian heritage. Early American settlers arriving from Europe set up breweries in their homes, and eventually started commercial production, using recipes inherited through family lineages. If you follow beer recipes back through the ages, you will see all the major technological milestones in human civilization represented through ever-more-sophisticated beer-brewing methods.

When choosing a style of barley beer to make in the modern home fermenting kitchen, you need to consider a number of things. Do you want a higher-alcohol or lower-alcohol beer? How bitter would you like your beer? Do you want to start with whole ingredients or use extracts? Would you prefer a light or dark beer? If you are new to beer-making, darker-colored beers with simple recipes are a good starting point. Generally speaking, darker, more flavorful beers will mask several common mistakes where a lighter beer might call attention to them.

American pale ale and American brown ale are true American classics. Both are easy to make, and on the spectrum of beer colors, both are on the darker side. We make beer like we make all our ferments: using whole, natural ingredients. With this in mind, both these recipes start with malted grains that result in deep, character-filled brews. The other option would be to use malted grain extracts, which can be costly and leave your beer lacking in complex flavor but will allow you to skip a couple of time-consuming steps.

An overview of barley beer-making

Before making beer, you must wash, rinse, and sanitize everything that will come in contact with an ingredient. Cleanse and sanitize everything with brewer's grade products (PBW and Star San). This step is crucial, and if not carried out correctly may be the cause of bacterial, mold, or errant yeast contamination that will result in off-tasting or acidic beer. A good practice is to store your equipment in a large vessel of sanitizer on the countertop before and between brewing steps. You will also dunk your hands in this bath regularly.

Once your equipment is gathered and the brewing area sanitized, you will make the mash. In this step, the fermentable sugars will be extracted from your malted barley. Hot water, called "liqueur," is poured over crushed malted grain and brought to a specific temperature that is optimized for grain type. The starches will quickly convert to sugar and the result is wort, the substrate for beer. After mashing, the wort is drained off and the leftover grain is sparged. Sparging is the rinsing of mashed grains to capture all the remaining sugars. This final rinse is then lautered, or strained, into another vessel for boiling.

The boil will denature the enzymes that survived the mash, and this is when the hops are added. Hops do two very important things to grain beers: they add a fruity, floral aroma and flavor while acting as a preservative. Hops comprise two main acid types, alpha and beta. The alpha acids act as the preservative and microbiological agent while the beta acids act as a bittering agent. During the boil, different types of hops are added at different times that are carefully chosen to extract the exact amount of each of these acids. Too much and the beer will be too bitter; too little and the beer could spoil or be left flat in flavor. Hops are available whole, as they are picked, or as concentrated pellets. Both will work great in your beer.

Hops have found their way into beer recipes far and wide but are a relatively new ingredient. Before the 1700s, when the English parliament made it illegal to use other ingredients to flavor and bitter beer (to increase their revenue through hops taxation), a variety of ingredients were used and resulted in a wide array of local flavors and styles of beer. Rosemary, spruce, ginger, heather, and myrtle were just some of the common ingredients that all but disappeared under this ruling. Today local brew shops and very thorough brewing guides are reviving the art of brewing with unique flavoring agents.

Once the boil is complete, the wort is then cooled, and sterile practices must be strictly enforced from then onward, before yeast is added, or pitched. Once the yeast is pitched, primary fermentation can begin. After twelve to forty-eight hours, the brew will start bubbling and looking alive. Aggressive fermentation will last anywhere from two to five days. During this stage, we recommend using a blow-off tube (tube inserted into the bung and terminating submerged in a jar of sanitizer) to capture and discard the foamy suds that issue forth. An air lock used in this active stage of fermentation will gum up with the foamy blow off. After the yeast uses up the majority of the sugar, the beer can then be racked (transferred, leaving behind yeast sediment) for secondary fermentation. At this point, some recipes call for "dry hopping," or adding more hops that will sit in the brew until it is finished. Secondary fermentation will take seven to fourteen days, and the beer will clarify significantly during this time. The final stage of a typical beer recipe is bottle conditioning. Depending on the recipe, priming sugar can be added to aid the remaining yeast in the formation of carbonation. Another variable to consider is that particular styles of beer will benefit more than others from longer bottle conditioning periods also.

In our home fermenting kitchen, we tend to make batches of beer in volumes larger than one gallon. Because of the time it takes to set up a new brew, then do multiple rackings, and then wait and wait and wait, larger batches are more satisfying. The following recipes are for a one-gallon brew and are easily scalable to whatever size brew you have the equipment for: simply multiply the ingredients by the corresponding gallons of brew you desire. If an education is what you're after though, a one-gallon batch is the perfect manageable size to start with.

＊　＊　＊　＊　＊　＊　＊　＊

AMERICAN PALE ALE

Yield: 1 gallon

2 pounds pale malt, cracked

1½ ounces crystal malt

½ ounce Cascade pellet hops

¼ tube liquid American ale yeast

⅛ cup honey

Vessel: 1-gallon jug

Duration: 2 weeks (primary fermentation), 2 weeks (bottle conditioning)

1. Make sure pot, spoon, funnel, mesh strainer and surfaces are washed and sani-

tized. Additionally, sanitize a 2-gallon pot, bung, blow-off tube, and the jug for the first fermentation. Make an extra 1-gallon pot or bucket of sanitizer to have on hand for resanitizing your hands or other equipment before and during brewing.

2. Mash: Slowly heat ¾ gallon of water in a 2-gallon stockpot set over high heat to 155°F. You want the water to be as close to the target temperature as possible. Use the heating time to get to know how the temperature of your water reacts to your flame or stovetop. Once at temperature, add the malt. The temperature will drop when you add the malt, so bring it back to 155°F, stirring constantly to prevent the malt from scorching. Keep the mash at 155°F for another 60 minutes, taking care to stir every 10 minutes and adjust the temperature, keeping it as close to the target as possible. After 60 minutes, bring the mash up to 160°F and stir constantly for 10 minutes. This will mash out all the remaining sugars.

3. Sparge: Let your mash sit while you heat ¾ gallon of water to 160°F in a 2-gallon pot set over high heat. You will need the extra water to make up for evaporation during this step and the next. Set up a strainer over a second 2-gallon pot and pour your mash through. Then pour the warm ¾ gallon water over the mash in the strainer slowly to collect the last of the sugars. Transfer the wort back to the first pot, again pouring it

through the grains in the strainer one last time. Leave no sugar behind!

4. Boil: Bring the wort to a low boil. At this point, the wort will likely start foaming. Reduce the heat to prevent it from boiling over. As soon as the boil starts, start your timer. At 30 minutes, add ¼ ounce of your hops for bittering. In another 15 minutes, add the reminder ¼ ounce of your hops for flavoring. At the 60-minute mark, remove the wort from the heat. You will have lost enough wort to leave you with 1 gallon.

5. Place your pot into an ice bath until the temperature of the hopped, boiled wort cools to 75°F, stirring occasionally to make sure the entire pot is at temperature. Once you have removed the pot from the bath, place your strainer in a funnel and place the funnel into your 1-gallon fermentation jug. Pour the wort through the strainer to capture any left-behind solids. Add previously boiled water to the jug to fill to the 1-gallon mark if needed.

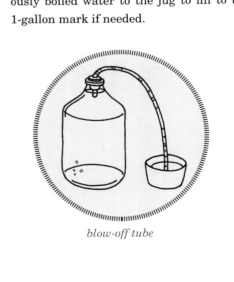

blow-off tube

6. Pitch the yeast into the jug. Sanitize your hand and place it on top of the jug, creating a tight seal. Shake it vigorously to bring the yeast alive and mix more oxygen into the brew.

7. Place the bung into the mouth of the jug and squeeze a blow-off tube into it. Submerge the free end of the tube in a pot of sanitizer.

8. Let the brew sit for 2 to 3 days or until the vigorous fermentation has stopped. Remove the tube from the bung and replace it with a sanitzed air lock. Put your fermenting brew aside at room temperature for 2 weeks or until bubbling stops. At that point, your brew will be ready to bottle.

bottle-capping

9. In a sterilized 1-gallon pot, mix the honey with ½ cup boiled water until it is dissolved. Using a racking cane, siphon your brew into this pot, leaving behind as much yeast sediment as possible. You will lose a little volume during fermentation. Mix the honey and brew and transfer to sanitized bottles. Cap the bottles and let condition for another 1 week at 68°F.

10. After 1 week, place the bottles in the fridge until cool and enjoy.

✳ ✳ ✳ ✳ ✳ ✳ ✳ ✳

AMERICAN BROWN ALE

Yield: 1 gallon

2 pounds pale malt, cracked

¼ pound crystal malt, cracked

3 ounces chocolate malt, cracked

¼ ounce Nugget pellet hops

¼ ounce Willamette pellet hops

¼ tube liquid American ale yeast

¼ cup honey

Vessel: 1-gallon jug
Duration: 2 weeks

1. Make sure pot, spoon, funnel, mesh-strainer, and surfaces are washed and sanitized. Additionally, sanitize a 2-gallon pot, bung, blow-off tube, and jug for the first fermentation. Make an extra 1-gallon jug of sanitizer to have on hand for resanitizing your hands or other equipment you will be using before and during brewing.

2. Mash: Heat ¾ gallon of water in a stockpot set over high heat to 160°F. You will need to be as precise as possible. Once at temperature add the malt. The temperature will drop when you add the malt so bring it back to 160°F, stirring constantly to keep the malt from scorching, and let it stand for 60 minutes at 160°F, stirring every 10 minutes and adjusting your stove as needed. After 60 minutes, bring the mash to 165°F and stir constantly for 10 minutes. This will mash out all the remaining sugars.

3. Sparge: Let your mash sit while you heat ¾ gallon of water to 165°F in a 2-gallon pot set over high heat. You will want extra water to make up for the evaporation during this process and the next stage. Set up a strainer over an additional pot and pour your mash through. Then slowly pour the ¾ gallon water over the mash that has been caught in the strainer and collect the last of the sugars. Pour the combined worts through the strainer one last time. Leave no sugar behind!

4. Boil: Bring the wort to a low boil, or heat until the wort starts foaming, and reduce the heat to prevent it from boiling over. As soon as the boil starts, start your timer and add the Nugget hops. At 45 minutes, add the Willamette hops. At 60 minutes, remove the pot from the heat. You will have lost enough wort to leave you with 1 gallon.

5. Place your pot into an ice bath until the temperature of the hopped, boiled wort cools to 75°F, stirring occasionally to make sure the entire pot is at temperature. Once you have removed the pot from the bath, place your strainer in a funnel and place the funnel into your 1-gallon fermentation jug. Pour the wort through the strainer to capture any left-behind solids. Add previously boiled water to the jug to fill to the 1-gallon mark if needed.

6. Pitch the yeast in to the jug. Sanitize your hand and place it on top of the jug, creating a tight seal. Shake it vigorously to bring the yeast alive and mix more oxygen into the brew.

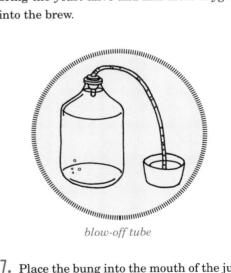

blow-off tube

7. Place the bung into the mouth of the jug and place a blow-off tube into it. Submerge the free end of the tube in a pot of sanitizer.

8. Let brew sit for 2 to 3 days or until the vigorous fermentation has stopped: the bubbles will stop coming out of the tube. Then remove the tube from the bung and replace with an air lock. Put your fermentation jar aside at room temperature for 2 weeks or until bubbling stops. At this point, you are ready to bottle.

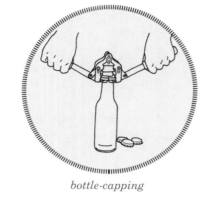

bottle-capping

9. In a sanitized 1-gallon pot, mix honey with ½ cup boiled water until it is dissolved. Siphon your brew into this pot, leaving behind as much yeast sediment as possible. Thoroughly mix the honey with a sterilized spoon and transfer to sanitized bottles. Cap the bottles and let condition for another 1 week at 68°F.

10. After 2 weeks, place bottles in the fridge until cool and enjoy.

CHICHA

Due to the way history is passed down from person to person, many people believe that the Europeans brought beer technology to the Americas. As is the case with a lot of what we read in history books, this is simply not the whole truth. Beer had been around for many millennia in the Americas, brewed in the homes of indigenous tribes. One recipe for such a beer that survives today is *chicha*, beer fermented from maize or modern-day corn.

Traditional chicha is made most often with Peruvian purple corn but can be made from any type of corn. Like barley beer, traditional chicha undergoes a process before the boil in which the starches are broken down into simple sugars. While most barley recipes call for malting, then mashing the grains to achieve this conversion, traditional chicha recipes call for the brewer to chew on the ground corn, mixing their enzyme-rich saliva with the starches and converting them to simple sugars. This idea—exotic and fascinating to some—further illustrates the interconnectedness of natural fermentation and the human body. But if this is not your thing, don't avoid chicha because of it! You can make chicha without the chewing step, as we have written this recipe. If you are in for the full experience, follow the alternate instructions listed in the sidebar.

Also similar to barley beer, a mash is made with the ground corn, which is then boiled and fermented. After the wort is made in the boil step, it is then cooled and other flavor-enhancing ingredients are added. Berries, cinnamon, cloves, mint, pineapple, pepper, or any other ingredients that might mix well with a corny brew are all fair game here. As with all our recipes, experiment often and report back!

✳ ✳ ✳ ✳ ✳ ✳ ✳ ✳

CHICHA

Yield: 1 gallon

1 pound fresh corn kernels (from 5 to 6 ears)

12 large strawberries

2 cups brown sugar

2 tablespoons lemon peel

8 mint leaves

starter: 2 cups whey, sauerkraut juice, or kuass

Vessel: 1-gallon glass wide-mouth jar with cloth cover

Duration: 3 to 4 days

1. Make sure pot, spoon, mesh strainer, fermentation vessel, and surfaces are clean and within reach.

2. Put the corn and strawberries in a food processor and blend until kernels are coarsely chopped.

If an adventure is what you're after and you want to chew your chicha, do this step after step 2:

Take a manageable handful of ground corn and strawberries and chew it until you can form it into a small patty.

Place the patties on a baking sheet. For a more traditional flair, let them dry in the sun; otherwise, dry in the oven with the temperature at 275°F for 5 minutes.

Continue from here with step 3 of the recipe.

3. Add the processed corn and strawberries to a scant gallon of water in a pot and bring to a boil over medium-high heat. Once the water is boiling, add the brown sugar and stir until it has dissolved.

4. Turn down the heat and cook the mash, covered, on a low boil for 25 minutes, then remove the pot from heat, cover, and let cool to room temperature. You can speed this process up by placing the pot into an ice bath. Monitor the temperature so that the mash does not get too cold.

5. Pour the cooled mash through a strainer into your fermentation vessel and add the lemon peel, mint, and starter.

6. Stir the brew once more before covering with a cloth and fastening with a rubber

band. Let the brew ferment at room temperature for 2 to 4 days or to taste.

7. Once fermentation is finished, remove all solid ingredients through a strainer and bottle the chicha in sanitized bottles.

8. Leave bottles at room temperature for 1 week to condition, then put in the fridge for up to a year. Serve chilled.

CHHAANG

Chhaang is brewed in the colder regions of rural Nepal and Tibet. A low-alcohol beer made from cooked rice, yeast, and ginger, chhaang is a pleasantly sweet, full-bodied, opaque white beverage that results from a quick and easy five-day fermentation period. In the warmer months, it can be served cold as a crisp, sweet, and refreshing drink. In the cold of winter, warm it almost to a boil and serve it hot in small tea bowls for a fortifying and hand-warming tonic. In the Far East, chhaang is not only enjoyed for its alcohol and delicious flavor, but is considered preventative medicine for warding off respiratory infections.

The style of Asian yeast used to make chhaang is called *jiuqu* in Chinese, *pang khao mahk* in Thai, or simply Asian yeast balls in the West. It is inexpensive and usually comes with the ginger mixed in, along with some rice flour. This yeast mixture is then pressed into handmade balls for travel and trade. Asian yeast balls can be found in Asian markets and online from a variety of sources.

We make chhaang in our oven with just the light on to give this ferment the additional warmth it thrives in. After the liquid chhaang has been bottled, we store the leftover fermented rice in the fridge and use it to make *changkol*, a tasty fermented rice porridge! See the recipe on the facing page.

*   *   *   *   *   *   *   *

CHHAANG

Yield: 1 gallon

5 cups jasmine rice

1 tablespoon Asian yeast balls

Vessel: 1-gallon wide-mouth jar with lid

Duration: 5 to 6 days

1. Prepare a clean surface and wash pot, spoon, and fermentation vessel with soap and warm water.

2. Place rice in a large pot and cover with 10 cups of water. Bring to a boil over high heat, then turn down the heat to medium-low, cover, and simmer until the rice has absorbed all the water, about 20 minutes.

3. Using a spice mill or mortar and pestle, crush the yeast balls into a fine powder.

4. Once the rice has cooked, fluff with a fork and spread onto parchment paper. Allow the rice to cool to room temperature.

5. Sprinkle the yeast powder all over the rice. Turn the yeast into the rice using a clean wooden spoon. Mix thoroughly.

6. Put the inoculated rice into your fermentation vessel and cover the vessel tightly with a lid.

7. Allow the jug to stand at room temperature (about 72–78°F) for 4 or 5 days. Do not open the vessel during this initial fermentation.

8. After 4 or 5 days, once the rice has compacted and 2 to 3 inches of white liquid has formed in the bottom of the vessel, remove the lid and enough room-temperature water to completely cover the rice and almost fill the 1 gallon jar. Close lid tightly again, and allow it to sit for an additional 24 hours at 76 to 78°F.

9. Strain the chhaang into bottles and store in the fridge until ready to drink. Stored at refrigeration temperature, chhaang can last for up to a year.

* * * * * * * *

CHANGKOL

Don't let that healthy fermented rice go to the compost! Changkol is a porridge made of the leftover fermented rice from chhaang. Its preparation is simple; all you do is heat it up. If you like, you can add some dairy, nut, seed, or grain milk or just plain water to get the consistency you desire. You can add almost anything to dress up this porridge. Something sweet like maple syrup will balance its bitter quality. We also throw in a tablespoon of extra-virgin coconut oil right before serving for its complementary flavor and health benefits.

Yield: 4 servings

4 cups fermented rice from chhaang

1 cup hemp milk, any variety of milk you have on hand, or water

Pinch of salt

4 tablespoons maple syrup

4 tablespoons extra-virgin coconut oil

Dash of cinnamon or cardamom

Chopped dried or fresh fruit

1. Put rice, milk or water, and salt into a small pot. Bring to a simmer over medium heat, cover, and cook on low heat until the moisture is absorbed, about 5 minutes.

2. Remove from heat and divide the porridge into 4 serving dishes.

3. Dress the servings up with 1 or more tablespoons of maple syrup and 1 tablespoon of extra-virgin coconut oil, the cinnamon or cardamom to taste, and chopped dried or fresh fruit.

TEPACHE

Tepache is something you will find for sale in its low-alcohol iteration at roadside stands throughout Mexico. Made from the starchy, inedible parts of a pineapple blended with sugar and herbs, tepache is an awesome way to use up those pineapple parts that would otherwise wind up in your compost. It is a quick and easy ferment to make at home, and when you do, your family and friends will be so glad you did. During the summer months, we make tepache on a weekly basis.

carboy with air lock

Tepache is very easy to make in both a low-alcohol version—blowing in somewhere between 0.5 and 1.5 percent ABV—and a higher-alcohol version that has the alcohol content of a small beer, between 3 and 5 percent ABV. Some recipes call for a bottle of beer to be added on the second day of fermentation to boost the yeast count and alcohol level. You could also simply pitch beer yeast into this ferment and let it sit at room temperature in a carboy outfitted with an air lock for a few extra days to drive up the alcohol levels. For the sake of tepache's heritage, we have included recipes for the amazing low-alcohol version that your kids can enjoy in addition to the higher-alcohol version that is exquisite on a summer night.

You can augment both of these recipes to change or add flavor. For a little heat, throw in a jalapeño pepper. For some relaxing floral notes, a few sprigs of lavender add a nice complement. One of our favorite additions is fresh mint. It imparts a fresh green aroma and flavor in the final brew.

* * * * * * * *

LOW—ALCOHOL TEPACHE

Yield: 1 gallon

1 organic pineapple

10 ounces brown sugar

3 cinnamon sticks

2 teaspoons cloves

Vessel: 1-gallon wide-mouth glass jar with lid

Duration: 2 to 4 days

1. Scrub the outside of the pineapple with warm water and a brush.

2. Cut the top and bottom off the pineapple and discard. Cut off the skin and remove the core of the pineapple by cutting the flesh away from it in 4 long slices. Keep the skin and core, and set aside the flesh for other uses. Cut the core and the pineapple skins into approximately 1-inch cubes.

3. In a small pot, heat 6 cups of water, stirring, to just below a simmer. Add the brown sugar, stirring to dissolve.

4. Pour 8 cups cool water into the fermentation jar. Add the warm brown sugar solution to the cool water.

5. Add the pineapple skin and core cubes, cinnamon, and cloves to the lukewarm mixture, then top off with water until the 1-gallon vessel is almost full, about 2 cups.

6. Tightly seal the jar and let rest at room temperature for 24 to 48 hours, but taste it after 24 hours. The tepache should be slightly carbonated, tart, and a little sweet.

7. When primary fermentation is finished, strain out the fruit and flavoring and either bottle, cap tightly, and bottle condition for an additional 24 to 48 hours hours at room temperature before putting it in the refrigerator, or, place into bottles, cap, and store in the fridge immediately, to be served and enjoyed with the light effervescence already present.

bottle-capping

If you let your tepache brew for too long, you make pineapple vinegar. Do not toss it; it's equally delicious and useful in salad dressings and marinades or as a pan deglazer!

MUST-TRY PIÑA GINGERADA

One of our favorite spiffed-up versions of tepache that we make at home uses maple syrup instead of brown sugar. We spice it up with a kick of ginger too! It makes for one of the best refreshing bubbly brews around and can be used in either the low-alcohol or high-alcohol version of tepache. Just substitute ½ cup maple syrup for the sugar and a 2-inch chunk of ginger, sliced, for the cinnamon and cloves. Fermentation takes about 48 hours, and we like to bottle condition at room temperature for another 48 hours before cooling and serving. The final brew will have small, elegant bubbles; it's semisweet with subtle spicy notes, balanced by a perfect level of acidity.

SMALL BEER—STYLE TEPACHE

Yield: 1 gallon

1 organic pineapple

10 ounces brown sugar

½ ounce whole cone Cascade hops

½ pack dry ale yeast

Vessel: 1-gallon wide-mouth glass jar with lid and 1-gallon brew vessel

Duration: 1 week

1. Scrub the outside of the pineapple with warm water and a brush.

2. Cut the top and bottom off the pineapple and discard. Cut off the skin and remove the core of the pineapple by cutting the flesh away from it in 4 long slices. Keep the skin and core, and set aside the flesh for other uses. Cut the core and the pineapple skins into approximately 1-inch cubes.

3. In a small pot, heat 6 cups of water to just below a simmer. Add the brown sugar, stirring to dissolve.

4. Pour 8 cups cool water into the fermentation jar. Add the warm brown sugar solution to the cool water.

5. Add pineapple skin and core cubes and hops to the jar, then top off with water until the 1-gallon vessel is almost full, about 2 cups.

6. Tightly seal the jar and let rest at room temperature for 24 to 48 hours, but taste after 24 hours. The tepache should be slightly carbonated, tart, and a little sweet.

7. Strain off the fruit and solids from the tepache into a pot. Siphon the liquid into a sanitized 1-gallon brew vessel.

8. Pitch yeast into the brew and, with a sanitized hand, place hand over brew vessel and shake vigorously. This will activate the yeast.

9. Put an air lock on the brew and let sit for 10 days or until bubbles stop forming in the air lock.

10. Siphon into bottles and allow to bottle condition for 1 week. Cool and enjoy.

GINGER BEER

Native to Asia, ginger has been an ingredient in Asian and Indian medicines, foods, and beverages since before the common era. As such, over the years ginger popped up in many recipes involving fermentation, but it wasn't until the late 1700s that beer brewed specifically from the starchy ginger root became a popular drink in Victorian England. From there, ginger beer spread all over Europe and to the Americas, where it was the predecessor of ginger ale, a clarified soda made by flavoring soda water. Before Prohibition, ginger beer was a common beverage alongside barley beer. Once Prohibition hit, breweries producing ginger beers all but vanished. Today, ginger beer breweries are finally making a comeback, with a few small micro ginger brewers popping up in the Northeast.

The basic ginger beer recipe calls for freshly ground ginger, water, and yeast. In our experience, with a little tweaking, ginger beer can quickly become a staple—and your friends will keep asking when you're making more. With the addition of pineapple juice and lemon (which have a magical flavor synergy with ginger), a little bit of extra sugar, and ale yeast (as opposed to airborne wild yeasts), the ginger beer becomes a beautiful concoction of bubbles, flowers, spice, and sweetness with an ABV of up to 9 percent.

* * * * * * * *

GINGER BEER

If there is one recipe you make from this book, make this ginger beer. It is divine.

Yield: 1 gallon

⅓ pound fresh ginger root

1 cup cane sugar

1 cup pineapple juice

1 tablespoon lemon juice

½ pack dry ale yeast

Vessel: 1-gallon jug

Duration: 2 weeks

1. Finely chop the ginger. There is no need to peel it. This will add to the body and spice of the brew.

2. Put ½ gallon water into a pot set over high heat and bring to 200°F. Add ginger. Keep at a low boil, covered, for 60 minutes.

3. Pour the brew through a strainer to remove large ginger solids.

4. Add the sugar and let dissolve. Add the pineapple and lemon juices and stir.

5. Place the pot in an ice bath and chill the brew to room temperature. Pour it into the sanitized fermentation vessel and pitch in the yeast. With a sanitized hand, place hand over vessel lid and shake the brew vigorously to activate the yeast.

6. Insert an air lock into the vessel and let sit for 2 weeks or until the bubbles stop forming in the air lock.

7. Siphon the ginger beer, using a sanitized racking cane and tip, into bottles and let condition for 1 to 2 weeks out of the fridge. Place the bottles in the refrigerator to cool, and then enjoy within 6 to 8 months.

MEAD

Mead, also called honey wine, has been made around the world for a very long time. In China, literature from 7000 BCE speaks of a honey-based elixir fermented with rice, fruit, and herbs. Literature from Ancient Greece around the time of Aristotle (ca. 350 BCE), talks about mead being served in the royal court and consumed at banquets. Simple, easy honey mead has persisted throughout the ages to arrive in our home fermenting kitchens just as it was when our ancestors first fell in love with it.

Referenced throughout history, in popular novels, and in modern films, mead is one of the oldest and most romantic of the fermented beverages. While mead is often enhanced with fruit, spices, or herbs, the most basic mead made simply with honey and water can be exquisite. Meads are sweet, semisweet, or dry and either bubbly or still. Anyone who has licked a spoonful of raw, freshly harvested honey will know that honey carries with it a romance of its own. Honey is made in minuscule amounts over a long period of time by individual bees that are part of a large collective. Sweet in taste and golden in color, when allowed to ferment, honey turns into boozy liquid gold. Mead is a drink that will soothe the mind and enlighten the spirit with every sip.

There are a variety of different types of mead. Mead made with honey alone is simply referred to as mead, but when you add fruit, you might call it "melomel." Mead made with herbs and spices is called "metheglin." The many variations on these mead themes each bear their own unique story and name. In this section, we showcase the glorious possibilities that honey, water, and yeast have when mixed together and allowed to sit. Use these recipes as a reference to try many intoxicating varieties of honey wine.

Traditional meads make use of wild yeast. The fermentation vessel containing sweet honey water is left open for a number of days to collect the wild yeast particles floating in the air. During this time, the liquid is stirred daily to mix and aerate it. The methods used to make meads of this style require more involvement and longer fermentation times, but the efforts can be rewarding with a unique depth that is almost impossible to achieve using packaged yeast. That being said, the potential for unfortunate results when using wild yeast is high. Instead of nice, boozy yeast ferment, you might wind up with a stinky, sour mix that will disappoint. To get your bearings, start with the modern approach, which is to use packaged yeast found at your local home brew shop.

Your choice of honey will dictate a lot of the final characteristic of your mead. Choose the honey that your palate enjoys because the honey's flavors will be front and center in the final mead. We will never forget the first time we tried a bottle of buckwheat honey mead. Its body and depth were more invigorating than any mead we had tried before. If at all possible, try to use raw honey. Raw honey preserves many healthy beneficial properties and just makes better mead. If that is not an option, conventionally treated honey will work just fine.

Yeasts for mead-making are usually chosen from the pool of wine yeasts, with white wine yeasts being the most common. They will produce a balanced body in your final mead. Our favorites are the Montrachet and champagne varieties, but there are many types of wine yeasts and all are worthy of trial.

Brewers and consumers flock to meads that have good body and higher alcohol levels, ranging anywhere from 7 to 20 percent ABV, because the alcohol is an important flavor component of mead. To make really awesome mead, the honey and water will need a little nutrient boost added at specific times during the process.

Making mead using packaged yeast does not involve many steps or take much time at the outset, but the fermentation process and bottle conditioning can take quite some time. For a really perfect bottle, expect three to six months of combined fermentation and bottle conditioning time. To justify the wait, you might wish to scale up these one-gallon recipes as we do, multiplying the ingredients by your desired yield. Believe us when we say that when you open that first bottle, all your hard work and waiting will pay off.

* * * * * * * *

BASIC MEAD

Yield: 1 gallon

4⅔ cups raw honey

2 ounces golden raisins, minced

1 teaspoon acid blend

1 teaspoon pectic enzyme

1 cup white peony tea

1 package Montrachet dry wine yeast

1 teaspoon yeast nutrient

½ cup orange juice

Vessel: 1-gallon glass jug

Duration: 8 to 22 weeks

1. In a large pot, combine the honey with 9 cups of water and bring to a boil. Allow to bubble for 15 minutes over medium low heat, using a large spoon to skim off any foam that forms. Remove from heat. Add the raisins to the pot and then set aside, covered, until it cools to room temperature.

2. Transfer the honey mixture to a sanitized 1-gallon jug. Add the acid blend, pectic enzyme, white peony tea, and enough filtered water to make 1 gallon.

blow-off tube

3. In a sanitized jar, combine the yeast, yeast nutrient, and ½ cup orange juice. Cover with plastic wrap, secure tightly with the lid, and shake vigorously. Allow the yeast starter to stand on a heat mat for around 15 minutes or until bubbly, then add to the honey mixture. Seal the jug with a sanitized bung and blow-off tube. Put the free end of the blow-off tube into a jar of sanitizer.

4. Allow the mixture to ferment to between 70° and 75°. During the most vigorous fermentation period, there may be debris in the blow-off tube. After 2 or 3, days once the fermentation has slowed a bit, rack the mead into another sanitized 1-gallon jug (leaving behind the sediment) and seal with a sanitized bung and air lock.

5. In 4 to 6 weeks, rack into another sterilized, air-locked jug for secondary fermentation. After 3 to 6 weeks, rack into sanitized bottles and store in a cool, dark place. The longer you go, the higher your alcohol content will be. Age for at least 6 months before drinking. If you can't wait that long, there will be more booze on the palate, and the subtle, beautiful character of this time-tested brew will be lost.

✳ ✳ ✳ ✳ ✳ ✳ ✳ ✳

HONEY AMARO (METHEGLIN MEAD)

Yield: 1 gallon

- 4 cups raw honey
- 1 tablespoon fresh rosemary leaves
- 1 tablespoon fresh thyme leaves
- 4 fresh sage leaves
- 6 fresh mint leaves
- 4 bay leaves
- 4 allspice berries
- 6 cloves
- 1 tablespoon fresh ginger, minced
- 1 teaspoon orange zest
- 1 teaspoon lemon zest
- ½ cup raw pu-erh tea
- 1 teaspoon acid blend
- 1 teaspoon pectic enzyme
- 1 package Montrachet dry wine yeast
- 1 teaspoon yeast nutrient
- 1 cup orange juice

Vessel: 1-gallon glass jug

Duration: 8 to 22 weeks

1. In a large pot, combine the honey with 9 cups of water and bring to a boil. Allow to bubble for 15 minutes over medium low heat, using a large spoon to skim off any foam that forms. Remove from heat. Add the raisins to the pot and then set aside, covered, until it cools to room temperature.

2. Once foam has ceased, add the rosemary, thyme, sage, mint, bay, allspice, cloves, ginger, orange zest, and lemon zest. Remove from heat and let the mixture cool to room temperature; then, using a funnel, pour through a strainer into a sanitized 1-gallon jug.

3. Steep the tea in ½ cup of boiling water for about 5 minutes. Remove the leaves and add the tea to the honey mixture, then add the acid blend, pectic enzyme, and enough filtered water to make 1 gallon.

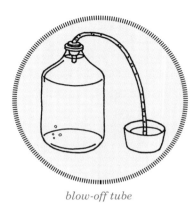

blow-off tube

4. In a sanitized jar, combine the yeast, yeast nutrient, orange juice, and lemon juice. Cover tightly with a sanitized lid and shake vigorously. Allow the yeast starter to stand on a heat mat for 15 minutes or until bubbly, then add it to the honey mixture. Seal the jug with a sanitized bung and blow-off tube. Put the free end of the blow-off tube into a jar of sanitizer.

5. Allow the mixture to ferment. During the most vigorous fermentation period, about the first 2 to 3 days, there may be debris in the blow-off tube. Once the fermentation has slowed a bit, around days 4 to 6, rack the wine into a sanitized 1-gallon jug (leaving behind the sediment) and seal with a sanitized bung and air lock.

6. In 4 to 6 weeks, rack into another sterilized, air-locked jug for secondary fermentation. After 3 to 6 weeks, rack into sanitized bottles, and store in a cool, dark place. The longer you go, the higher your alcohol content will be. Age for at least 6 months before drinking.

❋   ❋   ❋   ❋   ❋   ❋   ❋   ❋

STRAWBERRY MEADOW MEAD (MELOMEL FRUIT MEAD)

Yield: 1 gallon

2 cups dehydrated strawberries

3 pounds clover honey

1 teaspoon acid blend

1 teaspoon pectic enzyme

1 package champagne yeast

1 teaspoon yeast nutrient

½ cup orange juice

Vessel: 1-gallon glass jug

Duration: 8 to 22 weeks

1. Place the dehydrated strawberries in a small pot with ¾ cup of water. Bring to a boil and simmer for about 15 minutes, until strawberries have mostly dissolved into a jam-like goo. Cool to room temperature.

2. Meanwhile, in a large pot, mix the honey with water, using 1 part honey to 2 parts

water. Bring to a boil, and allow to boil for 15 minutes. Skim off any foam that rises to the surface. Cool to room temperature.

3. Combine the strawberry goo with the honey water in a sanitized 1-gallon jug. Add the acid, pectic enzyme, and enough filtered water to make 1 gallon.

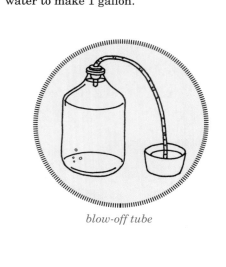

blow-off tube

4. In a jar, combine the yeast, yeast nutrient, and orange juice. Cover with plastic wrap, secure with a rubber band, and shake vigorously. Allow the yeast starter to stand on a heat mat for 15 minutes or until bubbly. Then add to the strawberry mixture. Seal the jug with a sanitized bung and blow-off tube. Put the free end of the blow-off tube into a jar of sanitizer.

5. Allow the mixture to ferment. During the most vigorous fermentation period, about 2 to 3 days, there may be debris in the blow-off tube. Then once the fermentation has slowed a bit, rack the wine into a sanitized 1-gallon jug (leaving behind the sediment) and seal with a sanitized bung and air lock.

6. In 4 to 6 weeks, rack into another sanitized air-locked jug to let ferment longer. After 3 to 6 weeks, rack into sanitized bottles, and store in a cool, dark place. The longer you go, the higher your alcohol content will be. Age for at least 6 months before drinking. If you can't wait that long, there will just be more booze on the palate.

⤫ ACKNOWLEDGMENTS ⤫

We wish to thank the following people: Jennifer Williams, Hannah Reich, and the entire staff at Sterling for their enthusiasm, talent, and expertise. Adam Chromy for his tireless efforts to get our word out there. Sam Dibble, Bertrand, Mama Bear, and Papa Bear Daubeuf, Emmet Moeller, and Chris Strait for their patience and assistance with recipe development and food criticism. Chris Bain, Bill Milne, Diane Vezza, and everyone who contributed their visual acumen and artistic and technical expertise to the design and imagery. And thank you to our families, who have always had the "guts" to support us and try our crazy concoctions!

⤫ ABOUT THE AUTHORS ⤫

JESSICA CHILDS is a passionate cook with a zeal for fermentation. When not creating or consuming her next meal, she is a science wonk who delights in questions that begin with *Why*. Jessica is a partner in KBBK Kombucha and Fermentation Supplies and has taught fermentation classes and has been on discussion panels at the Brooklyn Kitchen, Natural Gourmet Institute, and various Edible Publications events, among others. She holds a B.S. in biology from Bard College and a culinary certificate from the Natural Gourmet Institute.

ERIC CHILDS is devoted to creating and consuming beverages, with a particular fondness for fermented libations. He is the founder and CEO of KBBK Kombucha and Fermentation Supplies. Eric has taught classes and has been on discussion panels at Google Headquarters, Natural Gourmet Institute, and New Amsterdam Market, among others. He holds a wine certificate from the International Wine Center.

The Childs family lives in Woodstock, New York, with their two sons, Rider and Paxis. They invite you to drop by their family business, KBBK Kombucha and Fermentation Supplies, to talk fermentation anytime. It's just up the road on State Route 28 and can be found online at www.kombuchabk.com.

Also by Jessica and Eric Childs:
Kombucha! The amazing probiotic beverage that cleanses heals energizes and detoxifies

✑ INDEX ✑

Note: Italicized page references in parentheses indicate photo inserts: PP refers to photos of processes, and PR to photos of recipes. Example: *(PP-4)* refers to page 4 of the process photos; and *(PR-2)* refers to page 2 of the recipe photos.